SELF-EDUCATION
A Gandhian Perspective

SELF-EDUCATION
A GANDHIAN PERSPECTIVE

BERND PFLUG

GYAN

GYAN PUBLISHING HOUSE

New Delhi 110 002

SELF-EDUCATION
A Gahdhian Perspective
(Education, Philosophy)

ISBN : 81-212-0509-3

Published 1996 in India by
Gyan Publishing House
5, Ansari Road
New Delhi 110 002

Printed at Mehra Offset Press, Delhi-110 002

To

Leelamma

One cannot control all the consequences of one's action... But one must still think about them, and make choices.

Herman Wouk, **War and Remembrance**

The thing that plagued him was the inevitability of it all. There was the illusion of choice, the illusion of determining one's road. But the lines were cast by others and when you came to the crossroads the decision was already made for you.

Morris West, **The Second Victory**

If there were such a thing as absolute truth the debate would lose its lustre.

Penelope Lively, **Moon Tiger**

PREFACE

The purpose of this inquiry is to get clearer about some conceptual and normative aspects of a form of education which is self-directed by the individual, produced in deliberately conducted experiments and gained through experience. The conceptual aspects of **self-education** are those which are breaking up the self-educative process into features like choosing, deciding and doing. Its normative aspects are examined with the help of an hypothesis on what self-education ought to be. I shall propose to examine the argument that self-education is a means and an end following a humanistic line in thought and action.

Though Mahatma Gandhi's experiments with truth were not only a starting point for my train of thought but are still a continuous source of reflection, his example will only serve as an illustration for my arguments. This inquiry could have easily become a study of Gandhi, but then its material could also, as Kant had feared, quickly beguile the reader into an unearned acquiescence where empirical instances would distract our attention away from the sheer force of insights. This is not my intention.

That is why references to Gandhi will appear as excursory investigations only at particular junctures of this text in order to help clarify some arguments. They are not meant as allusions to a common thought in general.

But despite this I should like to speak of this inquiry as one undertaken in a Gandhian perspective, i.e., it demonstrates some principal features of Gandhian thought without following their each and every detail. It is even at times a criticism of Gandhian thought and obeys in this the Gandhian desire to examine ruthlessly to arrive at truth. It would be un-Gandhian to regard his pronouncements as scriptual truth, and I respect his wish to have no followers but to be his own and only follower. That is why Gandhi himself was against Gandhism. Gandhi has been ridden to near death many a time, particularly in studies by his disciples; so one more look would display either blind faith in his messages or a wish to experiment with thought. I shall claim to adhere to the latter.

This inquiry is part of the growing body of research into the philosophy of education whose recent popularity may be explained by what is being described as the increasing tension between traditional and progressive education and the uncertainty it evokes.

I should like to acknowledge with gratitude the contribution of two institutions which have made this inquiry possible, namely Kodaikanal International School, Tamilnadu, for granting me a Sabbatical of a full year, and the School of Gandhian Studies and Peace Science, Mahatma Gandhi University, Kottayam, Kerala, which provided a congenial atmosphere for my research.

SYNOPSIS

I. Introduction and thesis

1. A major function of philosophy is to help man remember. Remembering is not simply mental recall but a mode of asking questions. This mode is more committed to searching than to a body of knowledge framed in an empirically fixed linguistic form; it is seeing and questioning things which puzzle man behind their appearance of facts and thought. Remembering is thus an attempt to get nearer to successive approximations to truth.

2. The context in which this can be achieved is education. Hence a major function of education is to help man to sustain this ability to remember. Out of this follows that educating is then (also) philosophizing. Self-education may be considered to be the appropriate form for this philosophizing.

3. Self-education can be characterized as both, the process (or means) to develop self-mastery through self-knowledge, and the product (or end) which is knowledge of the external through self-reflection.

4. A thesis advanced from this is that self-education is essentially humanistic for it is intentional and rational in process and committed to freedom, knowledge and truth as a product. Process and product, form and content, thought and action are based in their relationships on the principle of congruence.

II. Self-education and congruence

5. Self-education as a product is a consequence of the acts of choosing, deciding and doing. Choosing and deciding are closely linked to thought-content and its relations in the internal and external realms. Choosing, deciding and doing are considered to be important experiences which are based on the premise that to make a choice is always considering its consequences.

6. The consequences of choosing, deciding and doing are self-educating and ought to help man become free from the bonds of irrationality. This can be achieved by allowing self-education to become political in its widest understanding, namely to rule itself.

7. Self-education contributes to self-mastery by way of pursuing the truth of a situation in productive association with one's social environment, hence to deal with problems of authority and power becomes a constant task.

8. If choice, decision and action are bound to thought-content, then there must be some kind of a pattern which may influence, and help select amongst, their relations.

9. The pattern advocated here consists of the concepts of congruence, experiencing and searching for truth. In it, experiencing and searching for truth would be employed to install a congruent connexion between thought-content and action.

10. This pattern of a congruent connexion is humanistic because it makes man aware of, and leads him to accept, the value of the unknown as something he need not fear.

11. This congruent connexion between thought-content and action as a self-educating technique is as interest-bound as any other construct of human thought and is thus ideological. It is an expression of the desire of man's need to impose intellectual order on the world.

III. Self-education and situation truth

12. The building-up of self-educating experience through searching for truth is a worldly and temporary process; it is also critical and historical insofar as it takes into account how past experiences have shaped man's thought by analyzing the driving forces which have led him to have intentions and to take decisions.

13. Situation truth is signified by man's efforts never to take things for granted but to examine them fresh and one at a time whenever there is a need to do so. Situation truth comes up with new insights and clarifications, all of them springing finally from a central agency, namely the compulsion to be moral.

14. To follow the principle of congruence means to act in a given situation in accordance with the newly found facts of truth which can make man gradually become aware of his potential and limitations and is thus building upon a healthy

foundation of scepticism a robust and down-to-earth estimation of himself and his surroundings. It is to make man aware of his own situation in life, his reality. To pursue this strategy means to apply the same moral label consistently to everything which fits the description of what is judged as right or wrong.

IV. Self-educating Experiencing and congruence-yielding

15. In self-educating experiencing man is guided not so much by new factual knowledge but by the humanistic quest to acquire new perceptions whenever a context deems it necessary. This occurs usually in times of crises and perplexity. Meaning is then given to the thought-concept by referring it to the reality of man's experience.

16. The knowingness which helps create situation truth is gained through congruence-yielding which is a form of knowing that is either a manifestation of a desire springing from knowledge or an extra-cognitive desire which impels man to know.

17. Congruence-yielding is self-educating experiencing. As that it is continually preparing the ground for a development of sources of morality through successive approximations to truth.

V. Conclusion

18. Self-education can now be divided into two components. There is first the self-educating experiencing which via the principle of congruence is the means to the end 'self-education'. And there is second the self-education which turns into a means while realizing the end 'moral life'.

Contents

1. Introduction and Thesis

A major function of philosophy is to help man remember.[1] *Remembering is not simply mental recall but a mode of asking questions. This mode is more committed to searching than to a body of knowledge framed in an empirically fixed linguisitic form; it is seeing and questioning things which puzzle man behind their appearance of facts and thoughts. Remembering is thus an attempt to get nearer to successive approximations to truth.*[2]

A philosophical perception, as any other perception, is already lost the moment we seem to have it. One reason for this is that, in philosophizing, we are driven by a desire to continue our quest for knowledge. Only if we ceased to ask questions, would we end up with a static position that could be regarded as a motionless picture which then could be argued about. Philosophizing is, however, of an on-going nature and any discussion based upon its findings can only be as temporary as the process of remembering. That is why any philosophical analysis can only be an entry point to a cluster of related ideas which change from one remembering to another. This may be labelled as extreme methodological pluralism in which philosophical thinking is an activity and not a doctrine, in which a solution is never final, and in which one of the main principles is self-reflection.

Applying our deep memory to problems of philosophy must not be confused with psychologizing where we would simply put ourselves on a pedestal of confession; rather it is to reconcile our deep memory with reason. This reconciliatory effort would give deep memory an opportunity to return to the mind of past experience with as much clarity as possible. In fact, this can also be understood as educating. Thought about thought is dependent on thinking which is an application of reason to deep memory, and thinking is always part of (self) educating. And to educate oneself in this way is the first step to educate, later, others.

Philosophizing is imaginative and historical. What this means is that we are dealing in philosophizing with our own histories and our own historical and personal questions and truths, shaped by our dialogues with like-minded people at particular points of the past. To insist in such acts on uncompromising arguments would in no way help an argument reach the state of creation. This state can only be achieved when the historical penetration is supplemented by the imaginative which is thus taking over the role of a complementary force. The Socratic doctrine that knowledge is reminiscence may be interpreted as a form of remembering that is not only based on bewilderment but should also lead to (new) bewilderment. Such bewilderment would be creative confusion about meaning, intention and understanding. As such, knowledge would be the successful source of generating new knowledge.

But do we want this state of continual philosophizing? Have we to remain caught in it forever? For the sake of our sanity we have to reject this proposal and have to ask how we can get out of it once we have accepted it as a potentially desirable one. What we probably do is to stick to our landmarks of thinking which finally add up to a philosophical position. This position would be a conglomerate of stable and tentative views and could therefore be discussed by everyone interested. But in this we cannot only go the empirical way which confirms, or not, by observation and experiment; instead we have also to go the grammatical or conceptional way whose positions are about the use of words and their meanings.

Word and world are seldom identical if at all, and we are tempted to read them differently ever again though we seem at times to be certain that we do make them identical by our thoughts and deeds. Since we are generally not used to questioning the meanings of our own words, we do not question the images we have of the world, and hardly do we have misgivings about our own remembering. We can only remember what is there, but we cannot remember what is not there. That is why we believe that what we remember is right, complete and true. This is a situation which is tempting since there is no one else who can remember what we remember. We finally assume that we cannot be wrong. And by so doing we are giving us some breathing space in which we do not philosophize but in which we are applying the landmarks and save us permanent philosophic introspection and analysis - not a rigorous but a commonsense approach.

Philosophizing is investigating into reasons for our beliefs. It can be turned into a justificationary stick, conveniently used whenever needed. But this would not help advance ideas and getting clearer about concepts and its textual network. If, however, identity of word and world is granted through (its meanings of) the use of our language, then an historical truth as a personal truth becomes meaningful for others and a communication reflecting only these truths is possible. The rigour demanded here is no less a rigour than the one required in an empirical examination. It is this rigour which insists on a change in us, if necessary, in order to make the identity work, for only then could we claim our remembering as philosophizing to be an act inviting academic discussion. This change is essential and encompasses our willingness to be open and self-critical in any discourse, whether it is in the form of a contemplation or public debate.

The despair about philosophy as a subject without clear answers is unwarranted and an outcome of an attitude born in the belief that a thing can only be labelled when it is fixed, clear, and submitted to a force by which we feel we should be ruled — whether we call this force God or centimeter. This unwarrantness lends support to the conviction that philosophy is not a system but an history, an open process which is not the truth but which is always looking for the truth.

Philosophy is not only criticism of the belief that things have to be static but also of any other belief and departs from this from a logical standpoint. It does not and has not to deal with the dissatisfaction it generates when its criticisms are found wanting, for example when they are not clear enough and devoid of certainty. Clarity and certainty are values of mere convenience. This does not mean that we need not strive for them, rather it is a plea for the acceptance that any process of philosophizing is only an attempt to arrive at clarity and certainty and leaves room for being challenged and changed. An attempt can also end in failure and delusion. Such philosophizing is also of a pedagogical nature, namely, the never-ending quest to come to terms with the complete objects of existence and reality on the one hand, and us, the incomplete subjects, on the other.[3] This rules out that philosophizing is regarded only as a technical instrument for the inquiries of specialists. We are well advised to acknowledge philosophy as a subject that does not provide ready-made answers which can be studied and applied but as an endeavour which contributes to the understanding of human existence and reality and may, thus, bring about new forms of knowing. These new forms of knowing emerge from two sources. The first is a critical and conscientious examination of a problem-situation and its underlying assumptions[4], the second is the awareness that we cannot simply cite evidence to resolve philosophical problems but that out conclusions have to follow, step by step, from some agreed-upon premises.[5]

The context in which remembering as an attempt to get nearer to successive approximations to truth can be achieved is education. Hence a major function of education is to help man sustain this ability to remember. Out of this follows that educating is then (also) philosophizing. Self-education may be considered to be the appropriate form for this philosophizing.

Against a great subject like philosophy, the cognitive status of education studies or pedagogical sciences is different. The characteristic problems studied in philosophy are of enduring intellectual interest, whereas the themes prominent in education studies are not of equal fascination to those who are not occupied with education on a regular and professional basis. At the heart of education lies the activity of forming attitudes and behaviour. Very often this is regarded as a natural activity which simply occurs and upon which outsiders have hardly any influence. Yet we know that this is not correct. Education can change the life of people to the better or the worse. Indoctrination and liberation may be used as trendy descriptions for these two possibilities.

If education may indeed by conceived as a continuous reconstruction of experience[6], then we need not look for a difference between the goal and the process of education.

And if we further recognize that the product of this process is education itself (our goal is to educate a human being to be educated), then the continuous reconstruction of experience will assume the form of remembering. Remembering would then be the goal, process and product of education.

Good education will give due emphasis to the recollection of facts and will assess this with the help of appropriate evaluation techniques, but will also put stress on remembering as an act of philosophizing. For the latter, two qualities of education are important, namely continuity and interaction. Reconstructing our experience continuously means to train constantly our ability to remember and to interact in this means to have the benefit of continuous reflection from outside.

Being aware of our own temporality and situatedness in the research process of philosophizing entails a healthy respect to any form of exploratory thought. Here we should distinguish between 'thought' and 'exploratory thought' of which the latter should always be accessible to the researcher. Mere 'thought' however, may be used for non-exploratory functions and may turn out to finally support rigid positions in life. If we favour any of these rigid positions in life, we must then be ready to face criticism from others who represent equally rigid positions. We find this situation not only, for instance, in politics where it seems at times justified in order to combat disasterous trends like authoritarian movements, but also in research where one ism is put against another. We do not advocate the abolition of isms - they are inevitable outcomes of human nature and provide man with the capability to build up systems - but in research openness should not be sacrificed and surrendered. We must never take for granted what others have thought before. On the other hand, the researcher as an interpreter of human existence cannot transcend his mileu; his work does not start from nothing, it does not occur in a vacuum, but it starts from the roots, and the main root is man, the researcher himself, his ideological concepts which so often assume the role of indubitable commonsense axioms. That is why exploratory thought is needed in research; it is called upon to acknowledge the temporality and situatedness of the researcher.

Temporality and situatedness of the researcher are signified by a knowledge of ourselves which enables us to distinguish between an existence which is bound to search and one which is tied up with the acceptance of daily life occurances. The awareness of our situatedness as a researcher places us in a role where we have to learn to make a difference between ourselves as a private person and, for example, an academician, i.e., a 'social' person . To be also the latter compels us to be open and to explore, to be only the former allows us to shut down our openness and relish in privacy, instinct and opportunities. This is certainly an unhealthy situation and should not simply be accepted as the price we have to pay for the two faces of man, the personal and the social. There is no reason why exploration could not become a widespread and common attitude in private life in order to fight inflexibility wherever it occurs. It is not necessary to take inflexibility for granted because it numerically prevails over flexibility. Exploratory thought might be a better tool for life as such though we have to admit that it may cause insecurity and anxiety since the grounds from where to judge have become shaky and prone to doubts in our modern societies. Probably everyone has to overcome this fear once we have begun to comprehend the process of the unfolding oppositions. The need to be sceptical is not to everybody's liking because it may question the very foundations of our existence.

Surely, one who is involved in educating as philosophizing has to take into account the problem that intellectual insecurity is part and parcel of his life. Educating as philosophizing is to do 'philosphy of education', the examination of cognition, desire and will (according to Kant[7]), and to answer the most important question, namely the one about the interrelationship of ends and means in education.[8] Educating as philosophizing is not craving for generality which would emerge from our pre-occupation with scientific methods, rather it is the inquiry into a human activity which may help us harmonize our self-regarding vital drives with (our) other-regarding vital drives.

Educating as philosophizing is also always searching for a subject in relation to time, namely in relation to the present ('What is the subject'), to the past ('How has the subject come into being?') and to the future ('Why has the subject come to claim our attention?')[9]. In our case the subject is self-education to which I have paid more and more attention in my life as a teacher because of the failures and shortcomings of other-education, particularly in the field of adult education. And given that this is so, it follows that self-education could play a much more significant role in education than it does today and that the "conscious formation of oneself is an important preliminary for educating others".[10] Thus, self-education presupposes other-education. It can even make other-education redundant if it refrains from the belief in the importance of systematic curricular instruction.

To begin with, self-education can be characterized as both, the process (or means) to develop self-mastery through self-knowledge, and the product (or end) which is knowledge of the external through self-reflection.[11]

There are two approaches to examine self-education. First it may be an examination from outside the person who is educating himself; in this case there is an observer who is taking down what he understands as self-educative procedures in the other person. As this he cannot be objective because he can only observe appearance. Second, self-education can be studied by the person who is educating himself. This does not make the research process more objective because self-perception is as incomplete and illusory as any other perception. But this approach can eventually become more authentic. Following the second way makes, however, the research process extremely individualized and the ideal of philosophical propositions applicable to everything that exists or may exist – the aim of any philosophical inquiry – nearly impossible. Yet we should not simply shut out a potential topic of philosphizing and its mode because it may allude set standards of research.

Traditional view maintains that a philosophy of education has to stress the research of problems of philosophy which are of direct relevance to educational questions. But this does not provide us with much of a possibility to venture into a philosphical inquiry of the 'script of one's own imprint' which is the analysis of 'old' knowledge. By this the researcher is asked to pursue both the approaches, namely to study first the 'script of the other's imprint' and then second to compare it to his own self- inquiry in order to arrive at a certain level of certainty and generality. This mixed approach of self-inquiry cum inquiry of the other could be used to formulate a principle, a thesis, a question, which then could be examined with the help of a 'model'. And so shall it be in this work. The thesis formulation and its conceptualization are acts based on self-inquiry which is always alsc an inquiry of the other because of its inherent element of comparison; its expansion or modification, will take place by involving, at certain junctures, the self-educative experiments of another person, viz.M.K. Gandhi.

While so doing, we are aware that we are faced by the problem of distortion of knowledge. This comes up as soon as the function of knowing is extended from self-inquiry to the inquiry of something or someone else by comparing behaviour and values. The degree of acquaintance gets vaguer the more we move away from self-inquiry. We have finally to admit that there is no neutral perception and therefore no neutral knowledge either.[12] In the humanities and the social sciences this price has to be paid unless our subjects cease to exist. On the other hand, knowledge generated from self-inquiry is more often than not hardly less distorted since our faculties of knowing are rarely clear in perception; on the contrary, they may be burdened by the desire of the individual to be perfect or to be right, not necessarily to oneself, but at least in its appearance to the outer world. The knowledge which is evolving from this desire may not be 'pure' which in turn may leave us with the rather depressing yet realistic outlook that knowledge of any philosophical inquiry may be distorted.Our task can therefore not to be seen in cancelling out distortion but only in the minimisation of distortion. This task can be achieved first by being as clear as possible about the source of distortion and second by having our reasoning so much under control that it does not slip away into intuition on the one hand (which would mean to compete with religious knowledge which cannot be our desire) or into tall claims bearing no resemblance with any acceptable form of reality, on the other.

That is not all. We may add that we have also to be aware of something which can be called the body-level of (self-) knowledge, which is a blending of the relations of 'having' and 'being', the mind-level of self-knowledge which is the intentional consciousness of becoming and which has "temporality as its main structural characteristic", and the spiritual level of self-knowledge which is the "transcendent poise of consciousness" of being as nothingness.[13] Without going into details of these levels of knowledge we may assert that it is far too much to hope that we would be able to secure knowledge which we can control at any time. Knowledge though often understood in the having-mode is in actual fact more in the mode of being, where the three forms of self-perfection, viz. self-realization. self-determination and self-integration , play a major role in the process of internalizing knowledge. May that be as it is, we are entitled to consider every knowledge though partial and relative as genuine knowledge which is important from the standpoint of life and human practice.

As any other form of education, self-education is at the same time process and product. This is so because to go through self-educative experiences means to be self-educated. To be self-educated means a) to have improved our knowledge base in whatever factual area and b) to have enriched our character formation at whatever age. The question arises whether the 'and' in the above statement is justified? For this we would have to find out which new knowledge would have a bearing on one's character formation. There may be a close nexus between character formation and the type of knowledge acquired whenever an object of knowledge could be turned into a subject: in other words, when something which is present to the senses has ceased to be something with marked qualities and attributes and has become the substance of reality. In more practical terms, we may say that knowledge contributes to character formation when it makes sense to the individual. But when does knowledge make sense to an individual? Probabaly only when it meets one of our open or hidden needs. But this is no guarantee that our character is being formed in a positive way. Here an active force is needed which can turn knowledge which makes no sense into knowledge which makes sense in order to function as a control mechanism. This force can be self-education which is producing sovereign knowledge and relative truth. As such it is then a means and an end.

Self-education is to educate oneself. This simple definition delivers a clear message of intentionality which goes beyond the "untutored reports of our thoughts, wishes, decisions and imagings" which are all intentional in form.[14]

Man who is educating himself does this on purpose with a specific goal in mind. And more, he might also have a plan of how to achieve this goal, i.e., there is some understanding of a method that has to be used.

We have to understand self-education in terms of what it is and not what it was. 'What is' embraces the past though, and there cannot be any 'is' without 'a was'. There is always something which we build up, be it learning a language, practising skills, or conceiving an idea. Though we may not call this determinism, it is, however, an awareness of the foundations we base our whole life upon. That makes it important to solve the problem of how to get to the past. By trying so in self-education, that is 'living thinking' as remembering, we are faced with the obstacle of self-centredness. Though we are willing to explore our self's past, we are so involved with our present self that an eventual clearer view on the past self is clouded by our present desires and needs. We can never go fully back to the past, neither empirically nor intellectually, and we are not able to reenact the past.[15] What we can do is to remember, but we should be clear about the fact that this remembering is not the past. Thus our knowledge of our own past is not the past itself and therefore partly elusive.

We are grasping only some of the past in everything what we are doing or thinking.— Thus it is impaired also in its dimension towards the future, and we are not capable of predicting that our self-education will lead to the wanted result. We can certainly make predictions but would be well advised not to declare them true. So what about self-education as sovereign knowledge and relative truth?

In self-education we can claim sovereign knowledge and relative truth only for the moment. The knowledge and truth we acquire in the process of educating ourselves is meant to be for a specific time only-as any knowledge and truth porcessed by man. To declare any knowledge universal would mean to deny time its temporary character. But this momentory character of self-education is not a negative restriction, rather it is an asset as soon as we have accepted this condition of the fleeting nature of time and self-education. This condition will remind us that we have to build up sovereign knowledge anew time and again, that we cannot store it without altering it, and that we cannot rest on knowledge we have once acquired. To fix knowledge for academic purposes may be legitimate and necessary, but fixed knowledge alone would not serve the purpose of the intention to aspire for relative truth; relative truth would have also to be gained over and over again. Such an attitude towards fixed knowledge is the most essential condition for the process of mastering oneself. It also means that we finally and solely have to rely upon ourselves as creators of sovereign knowledge in which mere learning of facts is not enough at all but in which we have to be able to work with what we have learned, either in applying it to situations or casting the situations to our knowledge. Thus knowledge in self-education is instrumental to achieve self-mastery of a situation. To realize this we have to refer to self-control which, eventually, may help us become morally better. This in turn would promote an increase in self-control of our actions and in rationality of our moral thinking. Being rational is being consistent, and being consistent in our efforts for self-mastery means to possess abilities to carry into practice what we decide should be done.

Here we could object that this understanding is a-social and would consequently breed selfishness and self-serving targets. This objection is valid unless we are able to give self-education a direction which makes it also (an instrument for) part of a design of a socio-political strategy. Such a strategy would be based on the acknowledgement that the power of the self should be amplified through self-education, that is through systematic training of attributes and qualities which constitute the self. Most important amongst them would be the abilities to think critically, to sense socially, and to act politically. Self-education which is nurtured along these lines would eventually contribute to an empowerment of people which starts and rests with the individual but which soon branches out to other groups and communities. The self as a foundation of, and a contributor to, social development would need this reflexive education in order to exploit its potential and to refine its strategies. Here we should be aware of the clear distinction between self-study and self-education. The first one is following a course of study through independent learning (in an extended way learning with a teacher though), the second is also exploratory thought on one's motifs, actions and moral values. In this inquiry we are putting more emphasis on the latter. However, learning in self-study courses must not be underrated since it is a formidable means of breaking the monopoly and monotony of other-education and should thus be always an integral part of self-education.[16]

Out of the above I wish to advance the hypothesis that self-education is essentially humanistic for it is intentional and rational in process and committed to freedom, knowledge and truth as a product. Process and product, form and content, thought and action are based in their relationships on the principle on congruence.

There is the age-old problem of humankind of how to become perfect. Religions have been founded to help realize this desire, and so have other ideologies. Accepting their concern as a genuine challenge, we have to admit though that there is no state of complete perfection in human life. The term 'perfection' can be replaced by 'balance', 'harmony', 'enlightenment' and so forth, without changing the problem. When we ask the question what is perfect, we must already know what perfection is, for otherwise we would not be seeking what it is.[17] However, the desire itself to become perfect is already an indication that full perfection is not possible. Only with no desire to be perfect would there be a full conceivability of being perfect. But as long as the question, the desire, the quest exist, so long will there be a striving for perfection. It is perhaps a futile question, but it is helpful that it prevails because it reminds us of of our own endless imperfection. And this is the first humanistic characteristic of human life, the incompleteness in our becoming, the knowing of it, the accepting of it as unavoidable, and the certainty that we need not pity our existence for it. Here self-education could step in to let us deal with whatever question and desire is there, although it would lead finally to the inevitable acceptance of imperfection. We have to be satisfied with this.

Out of this follows that we shall always live in a state of in-between: in-between the known and the unknown, the good and the evil, the beautiful and the ugly, the living and the dead. Because of this, we are tempted to see and judge a problem from our personal angle. We know this but we need not feel bad about it since most of us are aware that we are living in-between values and know that we have a duty to choose, the more carefully the better but nevertheless being also aware that this choosing is never the final word. Our answers to problems and questions are virtually our own answers and our actions are practically our own actions. And this is the second humanistic characteristic of human life: we dominate our own existence, we make our own existence, and we care not about its finiteness. For this we have to re-discover a language which is built around the realities of self-attention. We are attending to our existence whatever the ups and downs are; they happen only to us and to nobody else.

Self-education may help us cope with both these

humanistic characteristics of life. 'Coping with' would entail the realization of the characteristics to an extent that man is in a comfortable state with his incompleteness and finiteness as well as the critical examination of all the aspects of these two characteristics. Knowing the incompleteness of our existence is a challenge to our rationality. Should we fill the incomplete with something mysterious or not? Religion was and is the answer for the irrational in which man would be an object of belief and not on object of knowledge.[18] Acceptance of the incomplete was and is the reply of the rational. However, acceptance of the incomplete does not mean to resign ourselves to a status quo. On the contrary, this acceptance means to see a purpose in completeness as a lifelong quality; the purpose may be to change incompleteness into other forms of incompleteness which suit us more in a particular situation. Such a change can be attempted in any field of life, from a betterment in our vocation to an improvement in our moral ideas and behaviour. Intentionally we do perceive the rational situation as a summon to action. And this rational action is the first major constituent of our thesis that self-education is essentially humanistic in process.

The second major constituent is related to the humanist axiology of freedom, knowledge and truth. Freedom is the liberty to consent to the unfinished, unaccomplished and fragmentary. It is the approval of an imperfect life, that we are mortal, that there is no life after life, but also that we need not worry about this. Knowledge is the state of awareness of becoming, that we are able to de-mystify our own life and permit it to flourish though we cannot explain it fully. Whatever knowledge we deem appropriate for this purpose we ought to acquire, either in formal education or in self-education of any informal kind. Such knowledge may then be called sovereign and "knows no finality".[19] Truth is relative or situation truth; in it we fulfill our needs to know, knowing full well that there is no way to achieve absolute truth. There is no self-evident truth, truth is not apparent, it has to be found out This provides the continuity of truth. Once it has been found out, it does not become eternal, since it has to be found again. That is so because the relative is historical whereas the absolute can only be metaphysical.

Freedom, knowledge and truth are geared towards humanness of the individual and his social environment. This goal can also be partly accomplished, but in this fulfillment we may create states of self-realization as the maximal development of all of one's potentialities. Though this is a physical impossibility, self-realization as becoming a part of an ultimate goal of education provides us with states of subjectively complete experiencing. These states are signified by the cognition that there ought to be a congruence between process and product, that is between the rational and intentional thought on the one hand side, and the action-oriented towards freedom, knowledge and truth on the other. In other words, content and form should match. This is the principle of congruence. This principle is a potentially humanistic value which directs man to strive for perfection knowing that this equilibrium can never be attained but that in his striving for it he may contribute to humanness in himself and others.

2. Self-Education and Congruence

Self-education as a product is a consequence of the acts of choosing, deciding and doing. Choosing and deciding are closely linked to thought content and its relations in the internal and external realms. Choosing, deciding ad doing are considered to be important experiences which are based on the premise that to make a choice is always considering its consequences.

Consequences of choosing, deciding and doing can be intended consequences of an action (i.e., results of an action) or unintended consequences of an action.[1] Choice between alternatives is constantly required and a fundamental of the good life for which the only authority is the individual himself. Choosing is a mental act which is neither true nor false as an act but which while identifying the choosable is already value-laden and therefore not any more neutral.[2] Values are "rooted in human historicity" and are to be released through acts".[3] The same applies to deciding which limits doing to the chosen.[4]

The structure of self-education (as a process) is constituted by these three acts (of choosing, deciding and doing). Educating oneself occurs a) during the acts of choosing and deciding and b) while doing and experiencing the consequences of this doing. Experiencing is an empirical concept "that is derived from the relation of causality which is an empirical relation. Whether or not X is a consequence of Y can be known only by experience."[5] The question of precedence and consequence can be called secondary. What is a consequence for òne action is the precedence for another or, more precise, for the thought-content involved in choosing and deciding.

Now what is happening during these acts? The answer is: something which can be understood as the core of self-education, viz. knowing and willing. First, it is knowing about alternatives, i.e., it is knowing alternatives; and second it is willing to choose, i.e., it is the process of voluntary choice. Since willing is part of knowing, a cycle of activities is thus formed from knowing to knowing: this cycle is a manifestation of self-edcucation. A self-educative action means an occurence parallel to one of these activities; to become self-educated would mean to experience self-education virtually after each and every activity, and to be aware of this. So we would have knowing$_1$ + experiencing, willing$_1$ + experincing$_1$, and so forth. This action is again twofold: (a) reflecting after each activity on the activity and (b) reflecting on the outcome of each activity. This will make the process of self-education rather transient. Can we stop this transition at any point or other in order to demonstrate that self-education is not a lifelong enterprise? In fact, we cannot stop this transition since this would mean unthinking, un-perceiving and un-becoming, and we may well assume that these qualities are not existing in human beings. Only the degree of awareness can vary: but even the most constant or immediate practice is based on some kind of alertness. Negatively speaking, choosing, deciding and doing cannot exist without experiencing and willing; positively, every constructive effort in self-education depends for its success on the maintenance and strengthening of willing as a precondition.

The question arises now whether one of these three acts is more important than the other. We would well remember that in nature none of the three can assume a position of priority since they are simply acts in which one chooses (e.g. a book from a shelf), decides (to read it or not) and does (the reading). But is this the 'natural' sequence? Suppose someone has put the book into my lap, opened the page and is waiting for me to read it. But I don't do so because I have decided not to read but to take a nap. Have I chosen to take a nap or have I decided to do it? This shows that there is a degree of overlapping of choosing and deciding (there are many more than the one indicated), but there are also differences which make the above mentioned sequence not the most plausible one.

Choosing demands an action which distinguishes between alternatives, doing a rather than b. Only if there is a plurality of possibilities can there be an action which we have chosen.[6] The identity of such an action is determined by the intention of the action, namely either to affect changes in the external world or in the inner life of an agent.[7] Deciding does not necessarily demand this action be based on intention, instead it needs reasons for its action.[8] Reasons help make decisions between things which have already been chosen, in other words, the choice-worthiness of a or b may have already been established before. Whether this can occur in a state of "choiceless awareness" which would mean "an awareness which is free from all alternatives"[9] is to be doubted. It is also questionable whether it would be desirable since one of man's striking qualities is the Kantian "capacity for choice[10]."

If self-education is indeed consciously executed, then we cannot evade choosing and have to accept it as a challenge to our project of being which is made by non-reflective consciousness. Choosing, however, is reflective consciousness and makes us aware of the motifs we have. In fact, it is not possible for us not to choose, and even if we do not choose "that is still a choice"[11]. Whenever we want to do something which shall enrich our knowledge or awareness, we are confronted with a situation where we have a choice to do this or that. This situation of choice has become part and parcel of our life so that ever so often we do not even recognize choice as choice and not always do we pay much attention to the choice-worthiness of alternatives. To recognize choice as choice would mean to be conscious of something placed before us; this something has to consist of at least two items but is in actual fact often consisting of many more. To be aware of something would entail an open mind qualified to perceive each and everything and to examine it sensibly and critically. Surely this is impossible and would be overtaxing everyone if ever so attempted. It would lead to a permanent state of tension which after some time would be an impediment to be conscious and alert. This could then lead to the somewhat paradoxical situation that if we are always trying to be aware of choice, we shall be sabotaging the use of choice as choice by which is meant not only to enjoy to have choices but also to make them the base for appropriate actions. Choice as a value would dominate other values and perhaps result, in some cases, in running away from sheer moral pressure.

We have to ask now whether choice, understood as an 'absolute' value and a constituent of an attitude relishing in relativistic pracitices, is close to relativism which is without intrinsic validity?[12] We have to assume that the answer could be in the affirmative, because if there are always choices, one's choice will be relative to all the goals it represents. Then what about those goals which one's choice does not cover? If we do not take note of them, does it mean that they do not exist? Certainly, this would be a non-supportable thesis. On the other hand, we can sustain the argument that man is a product of alternatives he has not chosen. Instead, he has opted for a particular action at a particular time which ceases once taken, i.e., decided upon, to be an alternative. Deciding is thus the great leveller of the freedom of choice. Deciding though necessary, abolishes the alternative and with that ends the state of choosing.The action then taken is even less free whether based on reason or not. What appears to be a natural outcome from choosing and deciding is finally measured by its consequences, whether they are good or bad, suitable or unsuitable.

Now while choosing and deciding, we have already a prospective consequence in mind and choose accordingly: either the consequence will suit us or is desirous out of some other reason. Self-education is to control this process while at the same time fostering it carefully. Through this, awareness can be produced about consequences while at the same time the process of choosing and deciding can be led into a different direction. "The very willing is the doing", written by one Edwards in 1754,[13] might well sum up this situation where the potential cosequences are the incentives for the act of willing. This is compatible with the perception that willing is "some form of consciousness of the future" and that "the content of willing is distinct from willing"[14] in which the former is the end and the latter the means. We would want to claim that, in the light of this, the proposal to replace 'choosing' with 'willing' as a more appropriate concepton for an ideal autonomy makes sense.[15] Control of willing may finally lead to the realization of Kant's maxim of autonomy, namely "Always to choose that the same volition shall comprehend the maxims of our choice as a universal law".[16]

Another question arises as to which of the three acts is more value-laden. There seems to be no clear distinction between choosing, deciding and doing in this respect since all the three are equally connected to consequences and the awareness of them. The knowledge of consequences is limiting the three acts to a consideration where the future plays a major role. This relation may shape the course of self-education into either a relatively free or strictly bound form of self-mastery. All of a sudden, thought-content and its internal and external relations, the first referring to one's own values and the latter to those of society but not necessarily internalized by us, become more important than the precise functions of choosing, deciding and doing. And behind a thought-content there must be a value which is something like a reason involving desire and a belief that the action will contribute to the satisfaction of the desire. This value is in a position to stimulate the content and direction of a thought. The action following from this is behavioural manifestation. Do we choose, and decide on, this value? If so, then this would be a conscious and rational act signifying a freedom of will which would mean to be free to carry out our thought-content as thought-out decisions. Or are actions, sometimes at least, springing from sources which we cannot clearly fathom and describe? Are they based on a contemplative nature which "turns the self to itself and centres it on a state of consciouness from which its desire is to never fall and to remain for ever and ever" and which might finally lead to the confusion of the actual and the ideal?[17] If so, then our actions would be in fact re-acting to these 'deeper' sources; values would thus have an inherent quality of inducing people to actions; we have to assume this as accurate.

Given that all that is so as we have analyzed above, it follows that the consequences of choosing, deciding and doing are self-educating and ought to help man become free from the bonds of irrationality. This can be achieved by allowing self-education to become political in its widest understanding, namely to rule itself.

Irrationality can be caused by personal as well as social circumstances. These circumstances are conditioned by our way of thinking which in turn is shaped by our life in a community. These circumstances form a complex of values, norms and sanctions which acts as a platform for conditioning circumstances. That is why the process of choosing, deciding and doing in self-education is not only one of the mind but also one of a society and the interaction of the two. The chosen, the decided, and the done can then turn out to be good or bad, right or wrong in a particular situation.

The consequences of choosing, deciding and doing have to be regarded in their effects as self-education in relation to other structural principles of self-education. These principles are continuity, regularity, consistency, uniformity, stability and predictability. They help measure the effectiveness of a consequence. If a consequence is known to the individual as being consistently the same, provided the action is the same, then we know in advance what is probably going to happen and adjust our choices and decisions to it. This knowing is in fact anticipating. The same mechanism is being applied once a consequence is known to be occuring regularly, provided the action is the same, once its nature is consistent with its preceding actions, once it is uniform and stable against expectations. Whenever these conditions are met, the predictability of the consequence of an action is given, either low if only a few of these criteria are met, or higher when all or nearly all of them are being observed. The existence of these principles limits the 'openness' of self-education, i.e., the limit of self-education is marked by the ground-realities of the individual, whether he wants to go far or not in his self-exploration, or whether the individual regards success in a narrower or wider sense, or whether success is important in a particular field.

Within this high degree of individuality in self-education, to become aware of these restraints is already an act of self-education, and by pursuing a strategy of conscious consequencing the element of irrationality can be reduced. Irrational thoughts and acts may be successfully neutralized by this policy which is at the same time realistic and idealistic. It is idealistic because it takes into account the personal preferences of the individual, his desires and aspirations which are always future-oriented; it is realistic because it accedes also to his practical need for survival now. How strong this point is in self-education can be documented with, probably, everyone's experience of other-education where the consequences of choosing, deciding and doing are also a major element of a particular behaviour but almost always dictated by the action of the teacher first and hardly by the 'free will' of the pupil. In other-education, choices and decisions are much more limited than in self-education.

Irrational and rational behaviour depend on the interaction of the individual mind and the 'mind' of a society. There is a constant pull and push between the two, the subjective and objective in experience. There are the demands of a society and there are the likes of an individual. Harmony between the two is rare, if not impossible, because reason can only discover what is akin to it. A false harmony which is an enforced harmony and does not possess the concept of rationality does not help avoid the clash between the two but only makes it less visible.[18] It actively promotes irrationality insofar as it does not make an effort to analyze the given contexts of ideas and find out their mutual relations.[19] An extreme and ruthless individualism does not help overcome the basic bond between individual and society either. The situation is almost always one of antagonism in which 'the political' plays a pivotal role. The question is one of 'who is governing whom and how'? To govern is to be understood in its widest possible meaning as to wield influence over others.

What is the place self-education can try to assume in such a spectre? Formal education is widely understood to be a political activity which is generally divisive and perpetuating class differences.[20] Do we have to put self-education into the same category? If self-education presupposed other-education, then this would be a logical conclusion. But it is doubtful that this connection between self-education and other-education is so clear because self-education is originally rational and thereby depending upon the causal chain of thought and action in those aspects of human nature whose satisfaction brings about a good life, viz, intellect, emotion and will. Self-education would have the capacity to steer the individual away from becoming a lackey of his instincts and a slave of political groups whose sole aim might be to grab power. It would also enable the individual to go his own ways and not necessarily the ways of a group. This may be possible by empowering the individual to analyze the goals and actions of himself and others clearly. Such a role may allow self-education to claim a strong political character where value-judgements are being used every time the self-educative acts take place. Good and bad, right and wrong become thus categories which are adopted quite frequently and self-educative regulaltion could control their indiscriminate application.

Self-education contributes to self-mastery by way of pursuing the truth of a situation in productive association with one's social environment, hence to deal with problems of authority and power becomes a constant task.

Self-education is not self-mastery. It is first of all a means to something, a contribution to something, whereas self-mastery is an end, an outcome. Thus we use self-educative skills to arrive at self-mastery. The overall concept which assists in bringing means and ends closer to each other is the concept of truth, and self-educative skills are adopted in the pursuit of this truth.

Now what are self-educative skills? They are skills which are employed by the individual when there is a need for them. Such a need arises when there is a feeling of deficit, for example when teaching is considered insufficient, or when a situation in life demands an immediate solution or a solution which cannot be found in formal education. We tend to rely on other-education first because we are then not alone and confined to something which is known In self-education we are separated from the other; that is why self-education rests in aloneness, and that is why we resort to it only after other-education has failed. Thus, the first self-educative skill is to opt for self-education as a means to solve problems and to achieve goals, which means to feel confident enough to rely on oneself.

A second self-educative skill is to identify a need. If we are vgaue concerning our needs, we will not be able to identify ways and sources for self-education. A needs assessment can only be undertaken when we are able to perceive our situation, our reality, as critically and objectively as possible. This access to reality constitutes a fundamental alternative to a system that only purports to teach about it. Here, many complicated situations can come up in relation to the ideals of neutrality and self-protection. Clashes are unavoidable and solutions are inevitably tilted towards one of the two. Rarely is there a full accordance possible.

A third self-educative skill is, therefore, to learn to deal with situations and to analyze them not only impartially but also with a certain kind of detachment. This must, however, not be at the expense of our faculty of reasoning.[21] This skill enables us to see through the mechanisms of outside control which determine our life so much.

A fourth self-educative skill is the proficiency to evaluate our own progress after having tried to implement the solution. In so doing we have to face the formidable task to come to the conclusion that there is indeed a need to self-evaluation, and that not all what we think and do is automatically justified.

In sum, belief in self-educative power, the ability to assess needs, the capacity to design detached ways of implementation, and the proficiency to evaluate results, are major self-educatie skills. They altogether form the basis of what may be called self-educative competence. This is a competence emerging from a complex system of knowing and not yet knowing.

The most demanding skill, however, is fifth to be able to arrive at the truth of a situation, that is to perceive our reality with as much clarity as necessary and as much rigour as possible. We should start with the maxim that no one theory has the monopoly of truth. If this be so, then our choice for a truth is limited - but not relative. The difference between 'limited' and 'relative' is that the former is restricted to a temporal situation whereas the latter is bound to a cultural situation. The former is not out there (not only in our mind); the latter which is apparently out there is, in fact, only in our mind which has been conditioned to think as it does, through our identification with a cultural situation.[22] Situation truth is not always bound to culture, rather it is based on a perception of reality which is critical of one's own culture (as well as of others), which is taking nothing for granted and which is not forever fixed. We could, however, argue that precisely these qualities are part of culture, but I have to admit that I have not come across a 'culture' in which these qualities are consciously perpetuated.

There is nothing in life which is repeatable. We can repeat actions and say that we have the same feeling we had when we performed this action earlier. But surely we assume only that the former and the present action and the present feeling are the same. Instead, they are not, they are different, they are only similar. So the conclusions drawn from actions and their results are not the same either, nor are their consequences the same. We are so used to operate with particulars that we are inclined to take them as the same and turn quickly to a generalization accepting particulars as universals. But situation truth is not generalization truth, rather it is an attempt to examine each situation anew and afresh. It embodies the principle that there is no such thing as a disinterested truth of cultural relativism. Those who adhere to cultural relativism pretend to know the thought of the other, but this is not possible. What we may know is what the other person utters which may be only one way of expressing one of his thoughts. Thus we may know the expression but not the thought; the thought as such is not knowable to the other, but only to oneself.

Situation truth, instead, follows the directive that any concept we perceive or think of, exists - though we do not often know what it is. At one stage, however, we give such a concept content which, in extreme cases, only we can see. Say, if we invent a concept and call it mus. For us it has at this stage a meaning. The problem starts when we want to communicate this meaning to others; we try to explain it and if persuasive or powerful enough we succeed. Some followers are then there to propagate it and, later, the concept becomes a common one, either in a form fairly near to its original meaning or far away from it; thus a concept has been socialized. To see through or, at least, to try to see through this process is the task of situation truth. In other words, we must not necessarily believe in concepts but have to trace their original meanings and find new meanings in them according to the reality in which they have been used.

Out of this follows that a task of self-education would then be to enable people to de-socialize a concept if necessary. This can only be done in a social environment since it is only an environment which creates reality. More than other, very often this reality is bound to situations of authority and power on all levels. Now, how can self-education help people learn about these external dependencies in relation to concept formulation (belief) and rule (for which concepts are being used)? Two analyses are being required for this: first the analysis of ourselves in relation to our social environment, and second the analysis of our social environment in relation to ourselves. These analyses can make us see that most concepts are being formed while being socialized and not while being de-socialized. The former is via authority, persuasion and power, the second is qua spotting the structure of the first. This cognition is a judgement about ourselves as well as our social environment. We are either seeing it and choose and decide to act, or we are seeing it and do not choose and decide to act. If we do the former, then self-education will assume the form of a liberating agency; if we do the latter, then self-education will settle for the form of a perpetuating agency. If it is the former, then self-education is committed to the task of de-socializing in order to arrive at situation truth; if it is the latter, then self-education is at best a technique which makes the status quo just a bit more palatable. In this latter form it would not be much different from other education.

It is, however, important to remember that the function of de-socializing a concept is not a neutral process either. De-socializing is done in a social environment and, in any case, whether successful nor not, for a new social environment, hence it is part of an activity which is only possible because of earlier activities and because it is gnerating future activities. The world we perceive in de-socializing and the world on which we base our de-socializing are already imbued with concepts. That is why de-socializing is not liberating man from activities per se: we believe, however, that it can enhance the critical qualities needed for these activities.

If choice, decision and action are bound to thought-content, as we have said above, then there must be some kind of a pattern which may influence, and help select amongst, their relations.

Thought-content consists of the theme which is carried by thought-process. Here we are only dealing with the thought-content which is expressed. This thought-content is a fact which can be perceived by sense perception. This fact must, however, be re-interpreted by the observer while sensing the actions of an agent. (This applies also to ourselves as an agent and an observer in one person.) These sensations are either understood as fixed expectations or spontaneous images which do indeed need this re-interpretation to make them comprehensible: and because of this reinterpretation the conclusion drawn by the observer cannot be anymore 'pure'. To infer from the observed action via sense perception to possible thought-content involved in choosing and deciding of an agent is even less 'pure' since it has to go through layers of thought-content, and the way from observing an expression (the fact) back to the source (the first, original thought-content) gets longer and longer with each new choice and decision.

Let us now consider the situation of an agent. His thought-content which finally leads to an action is not 'pure' either. It is being (de-) formed from its first appearance to its manifestation in action. While forming sovereign knowledge via de-socializing concepts, thought-content is under, numerous influences from inside like desires, and outside like obligations. An essential intentional relationship between an object (that what is sensed) and experience cannot be fully assimilated in the process of experience, and it cannot be completely internalized in the process of knowing.[23] This relationship is determined by internal relations like interest, pursuit, engrossment, facination or concern, disturbance and distress which presuppose things being related.[24] These things do not exist outside relations and are always relations of things. Thus, relations are part of the process of inference, somewhat positive when it comes to be involved as such, but certainly obstacles when it comes to accuracy in judgement. Relations are by this in a position to help establish a connection to the first original thought-content, but they are also involved in changing this first thought-content several times before it is being expressed. There is no way that these internal relations are not determined or not affected by external relations which are referring to the material conditions of existing social relations and which vary from circumstance to circumstance while building up new situations for the agent. The two, internal and external relations, are indistinguishable from the point of view of an observer, and we cannot identify which has come first in a particular situation of an agent. But what we seem to know is the impact of both of them on the process of choosing, deciding and doing. We seem to have 'absolute' thought-content but have probably never touched original thought-content. We need the layers and filters in-between for our own socio-psychological protection and the protection of others. Privacy of thought depends on them. What is happening in-between may be called 'thinking' by which an object is distinguished from other objects. It is characterized by conceptualization and is much more judgemental than the first single thought-content. Thinking though can contribute to awareness albeit not always to correct awareness. Soon we are faced by a situation where we know that our knowing is rooted in having an intention and a corresponding action plan, but we should also know that this knowing is resembling the making of a decision with all its stages of socializing and de-socializing a concept.

Choosing, deciding and doing do not simply happen but need not follow a rigid pattern either (often they do this exactly though in our daily routine). If they simply occurred, then they would constitute a laissez-faire approach; in case of the latter they would help form an inflexible dictat supported by an uncompromising morality. However, we are searching for a pattern resilient enough to withstand the onslaught of both, the laissez-faire and the we-have-the-right-moral approch. With such a pattern the individual should be able a) to understand his course of action by tracing it back as far as possible to the original thought-content, to interest and dismay, and b) to establish an order of morals which offers a fair amount of consistency and versitality to take care of life in its manysidedness and resourcefullness.

Having found a pattern appropriate for this purpose means to have a yardstick against which the self-educative skills can be assessed. But not only this. Self-education can get directives from such a pattern: suggestions which point out what is important and what is not, clues to why to do this and not that. Self-education, which cannot be a substitute for moral standards, would need a supporting structure for its prime tasks of self-mastery, the acquisition of sovereign knowledge, and the de-socializing of concepts in order to arrive at situation truth. "Education becomes (thus) an enabler in the final analysis", but is also enabled.[25]

In this, the first focus of our argumentation should be an 'experiencing' that is the intellectualized process of the organisation of its raw material. Once begun, each experiencing fulfills itself in further experiencing and is signified by incorrigibility. Once made, it cannot be unmade. It can only be constituted inside social relations, but has constantly to stuggle between an 'inner' and an 'outer' activity. Since an object is never still, our primary concern is more with particulars rather than universals. In this never-ending conflict between subjective experiencing and objective knowing, thought-content and action will be the two poles which cause a pattern to surface. Since we are sure of a difference between thought-content and action, the need for a pattern or model does come to our mind whenever we think about our philosophical bases and the meanings of which no experiencing is devoid. If the two were identical or completely overlapping, then there would be no want for a design to help solve this problem. But since we know that there is in actual fact a gulf between these poles, in situations of everyday life as well as in times of perplexity and confusion, we may go as far as to desire a rationale for our philosophy on which we can base our choices and decisions and which would help justify our actions. By so recognizing our situatedness in experiencing we would also recognize the limits and possibilities of autonomous development. We would be able to perceive that very often a religious belief or a particular morality is taken as the basis for this rationale. They are as such not detrimental to the development of a thinking and free being, but as with any system they tend to become rigid by demanding too much from their followers. They are prone to chain them to demarcated beliefs and norms and punish them as soon as they violate them. No pattern would be completely free from coercion though there are shades of difference between a subtle persuasiveness and a brutal arm twisting. The pattern suggested here makes no exception and has to be viewed and judged with a healthy scepticism in order to prevent it from becoming a religion.

I propose to examine a pattern which consists of the concepts of congruence, experiencing and searching for truth. In it, experiencing and searching for truth would be employed to install a congruent connexion between thought-content and action.

When we talk about the matching of thought-content and action, it should be clear from the beginning that there is no complete congruence possible. Empirically the two acts are following one another and are never taking place at the same time. A sequence of thought-contents may make up judgements which lead to action, but time has inevitably passed from the beginning to the end of the process. Neither can a complete congruence be achieved in a community unless we could give up the idea of a society and an individual, being two different identites.

Thus, when we speak of congruence (e.g. between thought-content and action, but also of any other), we mean approximate congruence of content and form.[26] The unity of (any) two elements is relative and transient conflicts and contradictions inevitably emerge between them—and they invariably constitute each other's negative form: content into discontent (that is the incomplete), form into shapelessness or intuition which is claimed by some as the only way to truth.[27] On the other hand, approximate congruence is the state in which thought-content and action are rather close in two intentions: first that thought-content is steering the action accordingly, and second that action is confirming the validity of thought-content. This raises the question: what makes these intentions possible so that choice and decision can be taken by the individual with as little distress as necessary, at times even with great confidence? It appears plausible that experiencing and searching for truth are the activities which may create this setting. Experiencing in self-education is the activity which fulfills the openness of self-education, i.e., continuous experiencing is a guarantee for not becoming bound to one set of values and behavioural rules only. Instead, it is the cognition of an old or new fact with never ceasing curiosity which might then result in new conclusions regarding the fact. Throughout this, experiencing develops into, and becomes part of, a part of (our) sovereign knowledge with which we can operate whenever a need arises. Sovereign knowledge can also be understood as reflected experience accumulated for situations and time to come. In both the concepts—self-education and experiencing - the respective qualities may be exchanged, and we would arrive at reflected knowledge and sovereign experience. Whichever term is prefered, the one chosen will form the base for further cognitions. Self-education is such a process of subjectively complete experiencing.

If experiencing is the journey, then searching for truth is the content with which experiencing ought to operate. Searching for truth is on the one hand also an activity, a way, but on the other it gives this activity a clear directive for what it shall search, namely truth, and so binding it to content. By this is meant a truth which is the truth of momentary thougth-content. If we are searching for this truth, then the sum of those truths form one truth at the end of a judgemental process, and the action which is following is established with truth at its base. If particular knowledge-and strictly speaking any knowledge is 'only' particular knowledge is genuine knowledge, and I suppose we may agree upon this, then situation truth which is based on particular knowledge is genuine truth as well. But we would not claim this for more than a situation.

What could now be the motivating force behind the quest for truth? It is in actual fact 'willing' which makes a congruent connexion between thought-content and action possible: willing to experience and willing to search. Though both contain some consciousness of the future, willing is rooted in the present. But as long as present doing and consciousness of the future are depending on each other, a condition is created from which a congruent connexion can emerge. Without an acute awarness of the present and a consciousness of the future the value of congruence would be meaningless, since a congruent connexion has to be understood as a product of the present, i.e., a product which is being executed, but with a sense of future, namely that this product is being involved in something good.

A congruent connexion is not a unique creation which comes and stays forever, rather it is a connexion which has to recur in steady and rapid succession in order to make it quasi-permanent. It needs another (sixth) self-educative skill wihout which it cannot be created: the willing of willing or the intention of willing, a component of the nature of a human being.[28] Only if this is in place, then also all the elements of a congruent connexion fall into their specific places. A delicate balance has to be maintained though in order to arrive at a single thing which can be truly claimed as a continually produced state of approximate congruence. Put otherwise, it is self-education as a product emerging from tension and polarity on the one hand and from truth without disguise on the other.[29]

The pattern we are looking for may be conceived as a continuous reflection of the process of bringing closer together that what we have thought of (= thought-content) and what we have done, guided by the intention of willing. This will enable us to use experiencing and searching for truth as instruments of self-education. In other words, it is the yearning for a single thing while knowing that it is elusive but hoping what it is, or what it may be.

This pattern of a congruent connexion is humanistic because it makes man aware of, and leads him to accept, the value of the unknown as something he need not fear.

Is this now an 'idealistic' or 'humanistic' conception of a pattern? A major challenge to humanism is that it does not claim to be able to explain everything in life and that it is virtually reconciled with the idea of the unknown and the known. Not that idealism and other systems of thought and explanation are in a better position, but they pretend to know more, whereas humanism adopts a more humble position by accepting its shortcomings. Let us consider this question of the unknown a bit further.[30]

Man may find it hard to accept himself as what he probably is, viz, not a part of a universal plan or design but the product of an accident. He rather holds that he could always be different if the universal plan were or could be made different. He desires to be ideal or to be near to it. For this, he selects and uses knowledge to reduce the chaos around him to order and to understand the universal plan. At this point he is vulnerable to fall into the habit of believing that if knowing of the man-made is not enough, knowing of the god-given will fulfil his life and eventually change his unversal plan.

Man is, thus, driven to know. Our whole recorded history is an account of progress in knowledge and an interpretaton of our dealing with it. But to determine the limits of knowledge and knowing is a strength rather than a weakness of man. By not substituting something for what we do not know, we can multiply this strength. A substitute is often given the name of 'god' or of an equivalent. The unknown is thereby mystified and elevated to something special which has assumed the role of a maker of sanctions. Those who pretend to 'know' have become part and parcel of this game plan and are considered to be something special, too. In actual fact, they are employing an effective lever for gaining and maintaining power on a very worldly level though they pretend to be more interested in other—worldly affairs.

Institutionalized religion is the first to support and promote this process of substituting. It is abetted by an education that wants us to believe that everything is knowable provided we put enough effort into its discovery and acquisition. This way of thinking is sustained by an educational practice which imposes on man the notion that to know what is taught is good and that not to know what is taught is bad. Having gone through years of this kind of conditioning makes people desire to know at all cost, if not by intellectual than by 'spiritual' means. In the latter realm certainly nothing is provable which makes it in the end so convenient because this 'knowledge' is then unaccountable.

This line of argumentation must not be under-stood that a different education system would pave the way for a 'god'-less society, i.e., a society that is not afraid of the unknown. That would be naive to believe; education is anyway only the hammer which fits the anvil. To idealize it as a revolutionary system would be a self-satisfying plot by some who dare not concede that any present system of education is merely a brick in the wall of how to react towards the unknown.

The unknown was always a source of sacredness and scaredness for man; that is why he needs the myths of the past and the future for they explain the unknown in subtle imagination. With all our technological knowledge we have not only refined myths, i.e., we have replaced old myths by modern ones of our computer age, but we have also designed the means of how to deal with myths-and here the pedagogical have become more and more dominant.

But let us put aside the role of education in this process of mystification and let us examine the issue at its core: Why are we afraid of the unknown? One possible answer is that we feel unable to cope with values which are not sanctioned by an absolute authority. We need to be told that to kill is bad and to love is good. We are deeply rooted in the desire not to strive for conflicts (though we face them daily) but for harmony perferably set by an agency from outside, a government or a faith. We are suspicious of our own perception and reasoning and would eventually reserve these faculties for the natural sciences but would not employ them for the discussion of political or 'spiritual' questions. Where law and order have become key concepts, we cherish them in their various permutations and feel at a loss when we are suddenly in a vacuum where no-one is around to tell us what to do.

Ethtically and politically we are convinced that there has to be something absolute, whether in the form of a religion, a system of rule, or the weather forecast. We assume that this will give sense and meaning to our life and at the same time quench disturbing questions about human existence. A 'normal' human life is one long run-away from facing these questions and their independent examination. Routine and acceptance have taken over as mental and emotional safety belts. That some religions have become 'world religions' is but one indication for this state of affair.

But are the open-ended and the relativistic really so threatening? Is it perhaps because we cannot live with the insecure, the uncertainty? We are fascinated by studying the past to know where we come from, we analyze with fervour the present to understand what is around us, and we try to predict the future in order to be aware of what might be ahead of us. Even the present high-profile involvement in ecological matters may also be born out of an egoistic epistemological motif., viz. to predict what is in store for us in future. Here I do not mean to belittle the results of scientists who work, e.g., on factors which determine possible climate changes worldwide these and other works deserve all our attention; and here I do not mean either to doubt the concern people have for others this concern cannot be strong enough; but what bothers me is that even by caring for the planet and its inhabitants do we tend to operate with absolutes because we cannot bear the thought of not knowing or dealing with provisionals. And since some of us do not like to call the unknowable 'god' as an easy way out, we raise what we know to the status of an absolute. Even the 'god' less might thus be afraid of the unknown.

Every effort to substitute the unknown by an absolute, even in the case of the known elevated to an absolute, is not relativistic. A relativistic attitude would be when we did accept the limits of knowledge and knowing without any substituting the unknown by an absolute. But even this should not be promoted to an absolute either because there might well be other ways of thinking.

The relativistic attitude which is deeply humanistic is, however, of advantage in so far as it never stops man from knowing more. What we know today was not known to us, say, 500 years ago though the knowledge 'existed' also at that time. But it had to be picked up, perceived, seen, discovered by someone. In the same way, knowledge 'exists' today which we have not yet seen but might do one day or the other . There will be a time for it. On the other hand, there might also be a time for losing what we have already known. This swinging in and out of knowledge is what makes intellectual work so satisfying: to enjoy what we know and to discover and to accept what we do not know without substituting. Let there be all sorts of black holes, they need not worry us. One day we might find out what they are, but in the meantime there is no necessity, apart from a psychological, to explain it with something 'spiritual'.

The limits of knowledge and knowing are a treasure for they enable us to live in uncertainty. This has begun with seemingly simple things like names. For instance, why do we call a finger a finger and not an eye? So far we have not fully solved this riddle and many other though we have agreed, for the sake of convenience, on many of these simple things. These agreements help us survive socially. Yet we are uncertain in so many things related to our daily life. If we wanted to clarify them, we would probably fall from one despair into another. That is why we tend to believe, and that is why we tend not to probe and not to ask questions. If we accepted the limits of knowledge and knowing instead without substituting, we would plunge into areas where we could not simply believe. We were on our own. A truly humanistic situation.

We may conclude that only a humanistic conception of a pattern would do justice to such a humanistic situation in order to be in consonance with each other. This does, however, not mean that the congruent connexion between thought-content and action as a humanistic conception and a self-educating technique is less ideological. It is as interest-bound as any other ideological construct of human thought and thus an expression of the desire of man's need to impose intellectual order on the world.

This desire to understand the world cognititvely also contains the urge to find affirmative answers to the question whether the aims and techniques of self-education can be absolute and universally applicable, independent of place and time, culture and history? Indeed, they can, but only in our intention to make them so while being convinced that intention guarantees its implementation. This conditional intention is addressing 'appetites' which are the natural domain of an intention. This indicates that intentions have to deal with fleeting and arbitrarily selected topics; but this says only something about their contents and nothing their relationships to form; this relationship is always intentional according to Brentano's fundamental thesis of the intentionality of mental acts: "Every mental phenomenon includes something as object within itself, although they do not all do so in the same way. In presentation, something is presented, in judgement something is affirmed or denied, in love loved, in hate hated, in desire desired, and so on."[31] This thesis does not, however, support the universality of goals per se, rather it leaves it open yet considers it a possibility. That we prefer to operate with absolute values has its reason in the fact that we tend to believe in absolute ends, i.e., ultimate ends which are intrinsically good but which are difficult to define, a trend which has always existed throughout the history of humankind and, we may claim without being too prophetic, will continue to play a dominant role for future generations as well. It is the security of absolute goals, values, ends of absoluteness, which attracts people to strive for them. Hence, these ends are performing, above all, a socio-psychological function and are, therefore, not more objective or unobjective as any other relative end. This socio-psychological function is an expression of a particular interest and, thus, manifests a first ideological function in which an imaginary relation is installed in us as a connexion to real relations.

We are also opting for absolute ends in life because we may enjoy the system of absolute ends as it is, with its ugly side, its greatness of conservatism. Again a longing for security might be one of the major motifs to leave such a system untouched: a family in its patriarchal structure, a traffic system which 'produces' many deaths, a marriage system which may evoke marriage stalemates, a political system of an authoritarian character, and so forth. To keep it and to believe in it is easy since we find ourselves often profiting from such an existing system, either in terms of power or in money or in both. This would be a second ideological function and should demonstrate that no ideology does exist by itself.[32] On the other hand, we are used to work in other- and self-education with intermediate ends or "maieutic ends" which we feel is something worth striving for[33]. and which are being taken as prospectives of some other ends, both of them of a temporary nature. As such, the concept of end is neutral[34] but not when it is attributed to a value which it is-practically always—when being used. It ceases to lose more and more of its neutrality the more it is being socialized.[35]

An ideology is attached to any practical context of actions, meanings and beliefs, and vice versa, any such practical context is producing an ideology. By doing this we are attempting to impose an intellectual order on our world. This is a legitimate need, and everyone who does so is expressing a desire to make his world more intelligible and to install himself in an imaginary relation to real relations. Here we have a third ideological function which denotes that any thinking being is an ideological being. Being ideological is being social, in the sense that each ideological statement is also a social statement. And to be social is a sine qua non for human existence, and so is to be ideological. Just as no ideology exists by itself, so does no human being.

The problem with being ideological is not that

we are ideological but that we insist on our ideology as the only (right) one, that we close it to criticism and mouldability. We have to be ideological since neutrality does not exist. Full neutrality would be empirical identity and this is an impossible state. If identity existed, we would not need it as a concept. Being ideological means to interpret a particular thought from within[36], means to be partial, means to stand for something or someone, means to be on the side of something or someone. From such a position we would not insist on an idea, a belief, a meaning to be the final one; we would not believe in final ends, we would not advocate for a status quo but for a progressive view of life where, for instance, (self-education) is meant to be a vehicle of change and growth and, at the same time, be change and growth. Self-education within the context of a social doctrine is contributing to the use and advancement of a social doctrine.

Self-education as being explored so far has to be cautiously placed in this context because it can contribute either to the development of a narrow, non-reflective unconscious ideology or to a wider, critical, conscious ideology; it can become, and contribute to, reflective rationality which is the evaluation of ends as such. We should be aware that also the congruent connexion between thought-content and action is interest-bound. It is so in two ways: first, it is so because it socially exists. It is here, and this being here signifies a purpose: to make thought-content and action (more) congruent; and having a purpose is being ideological. Second, it is ideological because it is a carrier of relational content between the two poles of thought-content and action - and relational content is every new thought-content or theme which is turned into an experience through judging.

In self-education, responsibility lies solely with the beholder. This does not mean that it is anti-social. The agent is necessitated to, at least, imagine situations in his pursuit of self-mastery which include other people and situations in which he is not alone. It is not enough to know one's mind which is rather unspecific and can mean anything from how one can trick out a person to how one can survive a disease. It ought to be expanded to know the functioning of one's mind in an historical and a social location. At this point, we can explain why self-education is actually more difficult to be practised than other-education. We do not know the mind of the other but we have a chance to know our own mind; yet this does not give us an advantage of perception since this depends on whether we put it to use for something good or not. Other-education in its rather mechanistic procedures is often blissfully ignorant of the subtleties of mind, thought, knowledge of the other though its executors deal with these concepts daily. We know that in normal other-education the interdependence of the intellectuality of the people involved with the social and historical location of the knowledge being acquired by them is hardly being noticed, pointed out, and accepted as a genuine task. In other words, the knowledge used and produced in other-education, though ideological, is not ideologically explained, a disadvantage for every learner who has to be satisfied with so-called universal, eternal facts and rarely learns to put them into a system by asking the question: why is this knowledge considered to be important and therefore taught? Students in educational institutions do 'ask' this question very often, yet more in a grumbling than an inquisitive manner, and hardly ever are they invited to find answers to it.

In self-education we are bound to fail in our progress to self-mastery, sovereign knowledge and de-socializing conceptualisation, if we do not take into account the ideological function of knowledge production while setting up the congruent connexion between thought-content and action. Only when we are aware of the interdependence of knowledge claims, personal and social interests, our ability to will, and to reflect rationally, are we justified to talk of self-education worth its name.

3. Self-Education and Situation Truth

The building-up of self-educating experience through searching for truth is a worldly and temporary process; it is also critical and historical insofar as it takes into account how past experiences have shaped man's thought and by analyzing the driving forces which have led him to have intentions and to take decisions.

Experiencing is the foundation and precondition for experience. In experiencing we are going through the motions of trial and error, perceiving and reflecting, moulding and thinking of what we have sensed. There is much of this process which goes on automatically; this has to be so because many experiences are gained and made mechanically and are automatically internalized and thus form a shield of protection which is necessary for our mental health.

The other form of experiencing is more conscious; in it the individual is either facing a situation by accident or is deliberately creating a situation which is promising a (new) experience. In either case, the person is ready, willing and able to pond over his experience by turning over the gain or loss. The gain is what we have approvingly learned, the loss is what we have disapprovingly acquired. In either case does it add to the stock of our experience and can be used for future situations and actions. The building-up of a stock of experience is a lifelong endeavour and not limited to any place like an institution in formal education.

For the first time now we are turning towards M.K. Gandhi to illustrate some of our points. Despite the scepticism of Kant concerning examples in arguing I think that they can be helpful at certain junctures in order to make an idea clearer. Besides this, an example shows that the abstract is rooted in life which does not go only according to plan; it is life in which human beings succeed and err. Hence, there is no experience 'in itself'. This is why we need biographical knowledge of a life's course which provides us with information that does not figure in any curriculum.[1] What is such a juncture? For the purpose of this study I have defined it as a point of thought which is rich in pedagogical perception, which can stimulate further educational thought, and which can show the limitations of a theoretical argument in relation to human life.

Once Gandhi was called a "freak in the realm of Indian thought" whose whole philosophy was based on nothing but "plain honesty".[2] Other authors have characterized his way of arguing as "sweet reasonableness"[3] which was nothing but an expression of a one-track mind that ended in "moral arrogance".[4] Consequently Gandhi must have enjoyed his role as a "full-fledged guru" who conceived truth "to be magical-mystical, and not comprehensively through intellect".[5] Another author has critized that Gandhi "has used the first person singular with unabashed abandon" which shows him to be "too full of himself" and with no "time or patience for others".[6] Against these harsh verdicts we know of scores of writers who have come to just the contrary on each argument. Returning to Gandhi's own deeds and words the observer can be caught in the dilemma to agree with both judgements, the more negative and the more positive. Why is this so? May be the answer lies in this what can be called the great creative and experimental personality of Gandhi.[7] Gandhi experimented throughout his life, in England with becoming an Englishman, in South Africa with family life, with education, with his legal work and with public reaction to discrimination; later in India with new forms of resistance and construction, again with education, with questions of health, and the older he grew with questions of the ascetical order.[8] Our first question now is: How did Gandhi create a situation in order to experience?

Gandhi never subjected the terms 'experience' and 'experiment' to a careful analysis. Yet it is clear to an observer that he certainly was 'scrupulous' and 'ceaseless' in his experiencing [9]; in his own words, that he had arrived at his ideals which regulated his life "by gradual evolution" in which every step "was thought out, well considered, and taken with the greatest deliberation"[10]. Critics have judged this as an indulgence of an ordinary man who set himself "impossible standards" and who then tried to develop a spiritual power "to live up to them"[11]. Gandhi claimed that he was aware of the experiments he was to conduct and that he calculated with results that would enrich his experience. In this he was not shy to take risks and to acknowledge failures and mistakes.[12] When he talks about "certain conditions to making experiments", he means the five vows of speaking and thinking of truth, brahmacharya, non-violence, poverty and non-possession, and the determination to obey them even if it meant great discomfort.[13] These are fundamental conditions which are not dictated by opportunistic considerations; they are conditions which not only regulated his experiments but which were conditions for leading a good life. Nevertheless, Gandhi was bent upon the fact that he had to study a situation as much as possible before carrying out an experiment, and that only from a bunch of correlated acts an intent to experiment could be inferred.[14] Such experimentation would then fill him with "ineffable joy" provided "that love is the supreme and only law of life".[15] More than once he confirmed that he had "grave doubts" about his ability to undertake an experiment[16], but he countered this by regarding his whole life as a "series of experiments in truth".[17]

Perhaps the comparison that Gandhi, like Plato, "distinguished between how one knows and how one learns"[18] can shed light on Gandhi's standpoint how to create a situation in order to experience. When did Gandhi feel that he had to learn? Surely when he felt a need to do so. Immediately he could design a plan, a strategy which would help solve a social or political problem and which at the same time would be a situation in which he could learn. He hardly left a thing to be done by accident, whether it was a question of his own dietetics or of how to deal with a viceroy, rather he preferred the meticulously planned and executed experiment, i.e., he conducted his experiments deliberately. He was searching for experiments all the time. With this went an openness about his learning that is astonishing. There was no shame or shyness to admit to it. Failures and difficulties on the way of learning were regarded as stepping stones for new experiments in a manner which can be called 'clinical' or 'scientific'. This learning was executed with "single-minded attention".[19] But he was aware of the danger of being lop-sided and warned against those who were claiming "to be all-sided" but were in actual fact "only experimenting"; he considered this attitude "even less worth than broken almond shells".[20]

Gandhi's setting up of experimenting was directed by one supreme motif, namely that the truth had to burst through. "The quest of truth cannot be prosecuted in a cave".[21] People can only be tested in society and the outside world.[22] Thus his setting was implicitly deliberate, even when it appeared to occur spontaneously. It was secured in the knowledge that an active life left room only for growth but never for stagnation and that life was subject to constant change and development. Experience of this meant to know. Contradictions and inconsistencies melt away when there is this strong urge to experiment and experience. Then the ends become secondary, yet the means become an obsession and are "non-negotiable".[23] This is not to say that Gandhi thought so, but it is the danger anyone must face as soon as continuous experimentation becomes the essence of one's life.

Certainly we profit more from conscious experiencing by way of a succinct task, like Gandhi, namely searching for truth. If we are trying to apply this maxim to any situation or to as many situations as possible, then we are integrating experiences into the self-educative skills mentioned above; and vice versa, these self-educative skills give our experiences more directions to become gradually more conscious which can eventually lead to a semi-automatic status in terms of technique. This is the point where we have to be careful and try to avoid the trap of becoming rigid. It is well possible that the concentration on the pursuit of truth can become an overwhelmingly oppressive fixation which can assume neurotic tendencies. It is the intelligent estimation of a situation which can tell us whether it is worth to search for truth or whether it is such a routine matter that the search for truth would be a pompous affair and overdo the intention. This knowledge of cutting one's coat according to one's cloth is also part of the store of self-educative skills and is an important pre-condition to achieve situation truth.

To work for conscious experiencing and accumulated experience is to reflecting steadily on the congruent connexion between thought-content and action; only then can we, with a high degree of certainty, claim to have the right knowledge for a situation, or to attain higher forms of freedom related to the state of being or consciousness [24]; only then can we speak of the truth of a situation we have perceived and managed.

Four qualities seem to be essential for this:

1. the experiencing ought to be worldly, i.e., with no reference to ultimacy;
2. it ought to be temporary, i.e., once achieved, it is not gained forever and a new situation might provide a different angle and therefore another truth;

3. it ought to be critical, i.e., we should examine situation truth once gained again and again and scrutinize it from various viewpoints before making a choice and decision; and
4. it ought to be historical, i.e., we have to take into account past experiences on which the new facets of truth are built and shaped and try to analyze the driving forces which make us intend and decide.[25]

Worldly, temporary and critical attributes may be evident and clear: 'worldly' is a matter of temperament, 'temporary' is what is says, and 'critical' is again a matter of temperament, after all the three are of a somewhat fleeting character: to be executed and to be 'forgotten' then; they are like tools which, after having been used, are put back into the tool-box. But it is different with the historical dimension. Here we have to refer constantly to ourselves. We have to measure our worldly, temporary and critical faculties always against our past, how and why we have dealt with it and how and why we have used it. And even further, we have to use the historical dimension also for our predictions since to arrive at a situation is surely a choice and a decision for the moment but also one for the future: namely for our action which follows thought-content and judgement. Though this action follows sometimes very fast, it does so never at the same time, it is never identical with it. It is not a very far future, but it is not the present either. And more, in this we are not supported by our freedom to act as a causal power[26], instead we have every time anew to make it clear to ourselves that there is a possibility of choice and that the characteristics of these alternatives are known to us.

The historical attitude does not only put us in a difficult position – we have to address the self in us honestly and that may be not always possible-it poses also a more onerous problem to time. Since we cannot determine with any exactitude where the self begins or ends, whether it is rooted in what could be called the ideal Hindu self (atman) or in human community, whether it is more 'Eastern' as an end in itself or more 'Western' as a social object to others and as a social (and psychological) object unto itself – one thing seems clear: as soon as we understand the self as something special, it becomes an obstacle to ethical development.[27] Ethical development in turn is related to the past and the future by reflecting on a truth which takes into account both, the historicity and the predictability of a situation. Whenever our preferences change, one concept of the self may be supplanted by another; we may be one day more rule-oriented than on another and do prefer to allow the forces of spontaneity to take over tomorrow. As to time, experience is not repeatable (and we maintain that it is not), how can we then claim that an experience should be put under scrutiny as an historical phenomenon? This is precisely what we request when we are going through the motion of a congruent connexion. Are the other three attributes of being wordly, temporary and critical really a-historical? Would it not make more sense (as in the case of the other qualities) to 'forget' the dimension of time and restrict ourselves to the present? We would be justified to argue like this, if we continued to confuse a-historical with the self-educative skill of de-socializing. De-socializing means to minimize the social influence of a concept on us by comprehending and following its historicity. Such an influence very often makes us a prisoner of one special value;

some of them fall then into places by our acceptance and form later the unquestioned pattern of a culture, a system which finally steers us into a particular behaviour because it is socially so wanted. We would then not be able to strive for new truths, neither in present situations nor in future. De-socializing is precisely prompting us to do so: to liberate us from such a system of pre-fixed values by researching their social roots and meanings and feel free to discard them for us in a situation when we deem this advisable. On the other hand, de-socializing can also have another effect. It may lead to the vindication of existing values and their becoming even firmer in man's life. May that as it may be, the main aspect of de-socializing is its character of examination, its researching for proof of the validity of what is believed as good or bad. This does not mean, however, that we deprive experience of its historical rooting in ourselves. On the contrary, we have to insist on the historical method because only through its proper and regular application will we be able to trace our own involvement with the historicity of an experience. Once we are clearer about this involvement (active and passive), we will be able to free ourselves from this involvement to the extent that we deal with it and refuse being dealt with. We learn to see through our dependence on past experience while attaining new experience. 'To see through' conveys to us the point that we are at the beginning of seeing the newly attained experience differently in relation to past experiences, that is we do not simply accumulate new stuff but add a new reflection which we also have reflected historically.

Like thought, experience is not directly comprehensible by others but it is reportable. We may say that the act of experiencing is ineffable but we may also assert that worked-through experiences are open to the public in two ways: first in seeing the respective actions (though this does not mean much in terms of honesty and reliability), and second, through the reflection on the experiences which should stand the test of public debates. If we so raise the level of our experiencing, then we can experience ourselves in remembering.

To raise the level of experiencing was for Gandhi to match his words with his deeds.[28] Following this meant also to put himself under pressure. Small wonder then that there is substantial criticism about his endeavour, e.g. that he had an egoistic urge in him and that he had the manerisms of a "Hindu holy man".[29] As much as one can come to such a conclusion, as much has one to see the process behind. To have set a standard, perhaps an impossible one, forced Gandhi to put himself in the centre and to reflect endlessly on himself and his deeds. It is but inevitable then that the outcome is somewhat egocentric and even egoistic depending on one's standpoint of arguing. The outer form of this is then the image of the "Hindu holy man" who preaches detachment but who is also well prepared to accept all the paraphernalia of a very mudane and attached life. But here we have to give Gandhi the benefit of an explanation which has to do with what he understood by dialectics, namely a twofold process which cannot become static: "It is a process that takes place in the inner self of a person as well as in the minds of others. It is in one respect a Socratic method of dialectic in the form of debating with others. (But) Gandhi added one more vital dimension. It is debating within one's own self."[30] Out of this appears truth clearer and clearer and in an unambiguous form. "Gandhian dialectics is perpetual dialectics as it leaves out nothing"[31] and deals with becoming and experienced knowledge; it denounces borrowed beliefs and isms.

This Gandhian debating within one's own self is part of remembering, though I would not go that far and identify it with Gandhi's appeal to his "inner voice"[32]. But certainly it is what I understand as an inner struggle to arrive at truth as the reality of all forces which in turn enabled him to search for a self-acting freedom and not a self-determining freedom based on necessity[33]. Gandhi's remembering is a process in which our intellect is turning our mind inward[34] and where the heart takes precedence over the intellect. "The principle is accepted first, and proofs follow afterwards. Inspiration precedes the argument with which we justify it. That is why it is said that the intellect is led by one's actions. Man discovers an argument in favour of what he wants to do or has done."[35] And then late in his life (1947) he discloses (once more) that all his reflecting publicly on his experiments and experiences would not suffice if it were mere preaching but would have to be action in action.[36] "Mere thoughts act. They attain that power." But he was also aware that this stage in life has to be achieved through hard work; it does not come automatically that man "does not need even to proclaim his thoughts much less to show them by outward action". And he adds leaving us guessing whether this is resignation or hope, that he is "far from this state. All I can say is that my striving is in that direction."[37]

Experience so experienced is following the tenet of the Bhagavad-Gita. It is not the renunciation of all activities but the renunciation of activities "prompted by desire" but also the renunciation "of the fruits of action performed as duty". We may argue, with Gandhi, that while doing so we have achieved "real freedom from activity".[38] We may have thus raised our level of experiencing to a height which makes self-education possible. But it also shows how difficult it is to attain this state. In the end it boils down to the fact whether we believe (only) in the empirical self or (also) in the real self or atman. Gandhi was sure of this embodiment.

Situation truth is signified by man's efforts never to take things for granted but to examine them fresh and one at a time whenever there is a need to do so. Situation truth comes up with new insights and clarifications, all of them springing finally from a central agency, namely the compulsion to be moral.

Self-educating experiencing occurs while measuring it against a yardstick. There is no experiencing without this measuring because it is the guide to congruence. A congruent connexion between thought-content and action is only possible when thought-content and action are oriented towards a goal and controlled by conscience. Such a goal is rooted in morality, that is moral values function as the measurement for thought-content and action. The in-between, i.e., the judging, is taking into account these moral values while choices and decisions are being contemplated.

Whatever moral goal it is, we assume that it leads to truth or, better, that it is truth, and that this urge for truth would contribute to change. Nobody would agree that his goals were untruth. But what we cannot claim is that our goals form the base for absolute truth because absolute or ultimate truth is unattainable (if at all it exists). What this means is that there are many different expressions of the same goal-"these expressions have their truth relatively to their name, shape and function".[39]

Though Gandhi never claimed to be a philosopher in the narrow understanding or having originated any philosophy[40], he derived joy and satisfaction by "expressing original views".[41] One of his original ideas was his view of relative truth.[42] Unlike a rational humanist, Gandhi accepted the existence of Absolute Truth but knew that it was unattainable. He, however, considered it the guide that would inform man about his "choice of relative truths".[43] This information as part of a process of inner communication was also part of a product, namely part of the decision which had been taken on a content. Hence it can be labelled as "knowledge"[44]. Such knowledge could then accept any 'truth' as absolute as well as relative. Whatever nomenclature we prefer, one thing is clear: Gandhi was a realist concerning the matter of truth. He admitted that he was not well "acquainted with the Jain way"[45], but he used the famous Jain anekantavada or the manifoldness of truth for his own purpose. He never went systmatically into the seven modes of truth of the Jain concept and its definite and indefinite distinctions, but he used its general language to make his point clear that "My anekantavada is the result of the twin doctrine of satya and ahimsa."[46] Gandhi's use of anekantavada is primarily not epistemological but ethical.

Let us now see how Gandhi described his position towards truth. His approach can be accepted as a truly pedagogical one which I should like to portray as a humanist-radical since he could not give a guarantee that he would do or believe tomorrow what he did or held to be true today.[47]

Gandhi liked to question and to probe but always taking into account a standpoint "of whether it helps or hinders man's capacity for greater aliveness and joy"[48]. Though fundamental principles were for him "immutable", one had to accept the truth of other people as "bound to be dear to them"; consequently one should not prevent others from following their own paths.[49] His immutable fundamental principles were non-violence and truth. But in practical life Gandhi saw contradictions because it is impossible to achieve perfection. If so, there must be deviations from the fundamental principles, and to enforce harmony under those conditions would mean"to resort to untruth". That is why he recommended as the best way "to follow the truth as one sees it at the moment". Progressing so from day to day should make us free form the worry that "others see contradictions in us".[50] The truth of today has to be "tested in experience", but this experience is only valid for oneself – Gandhi never imposed his experience as "the sole guide" on other people.[51] In all, he advocated as the golden rule to "see Truth in fragment and from different angles of vision".[52] The truths emerging from this attitude are "limited truths" beyond which there is only the total, all-embracing and indescribable absolute truth which is God (or vice versa). Since all else is unreal and false, all other things could be therefore only true "in a relative sense"[53]. Relative truth which is thus fragmented, limited, many-sided and plural is nonetheless "the whole truth for a given time".[54] In its alertness to ontic truth, that is truth as concerned with fact[55], Gandhi's is a Philosophy of Becoming in the true Jain sense in which "what is incessantly changing is real"[56]. This is further corroborated by his belief "that we would not be deprived of the truth by the energy with which we immerse ourselves in a truth"[57]. Energy could be conserved and the validity of the fragmentariness of respective visions of truth could be confirmed by following a series of disciplines (margas)[58].

There is a deep pedagogical streak in Gandhi. Often it is impossible to decide whether some of his utterances are epistemological or pedagogical. They appear sometimes as a clever blend of the two, for example in the case when he suggests that truth-seekers must have this position also: "Just as there is acceptance so is there rejection of a thing. Similarly there can be neither rejection nor acceptance."[59] Since he was not very much concerned with epistemological or logical enquiries and was stressing action rather than thought[60], we may well conclude that his prime interest was to move things, to set them straight, and to change them.

But Gandhi was not above the danger everyone finds himself in who makes a distinction between absolute and relative truth. This danger is to hold to what one calls relative truth "with considerable dogmatism and inflexibility"[61]. Even the adherence to the principle of relative truth is somewhat absolute, and Gandhi's recommendation to believe only the latest what he has said or written in order to avoid the trap of inconsistencies[62], can sometimes leave accountability a victim. As a self-educative endeavour Gandhi's approach seems to be very valuable indeed because it allows growth to happen unhampered by constrainsts from outside. But Gandhi who was as public a figure as he was a stubborn self did at times contribute with his 'attitude of the latest' to the confusion of those he wanted to educate.

Like Gandhi, we are asking for situation truth as our yardstick which then is subject to change whenever a new goal has come up or a new situation has arisen. Situation truth is, however, to follow the principle of non-contradiction[63] and its explanations should be as true as we can possibly make them in terms of their correspondence with objective facts. In this sense, situation truth is a state of affair which is real and relative at the same time. It is real insofar as it does not claim to know the way to ultimacy or even to be the ultimate; it is also dealing with real situations which are being faced by the individual now and not tomorrow (though situation truth has certainly also a bearing on the future by assigning 'situation' to its demand). Considerations related to eternity, universality and invariability are not as important as they are in other concepts of truth, for example in genuinely Buddhist notions which then would be neither true nor false empirically[64]. Consequently, situation truth would not be an outside factuality. But it is also relative because it accepts the truth of different situations as plausible and appropriate, truths which have become personal, and so they are also historical. Furthermore, its causal relations are essentially temporal relations. Thus, it is realistic and relative in space and time.

If one is to pursue the truth of a situation, one has to be ready for experiments and experience. In other words, no truth is being achieved in a linear and undisturbed way. Instead, we have to search for it, we have to take risks, we have to change the course of our attempts if necessary, and we have to be willing to admit errors; in short, we have to be ready to question ourselves in every situation. But this leads to a number of questions.

First, who compels us to pursue the truth of a situation by experimenting? Can the answer be as simple as that situation truth is committed to experimentation? But this does not appear overly convincing because situation truth could also be pursued by using the same yardstick for new situations without experimenting. I propose an answer which seems more fitting: Compulsion for situation truth is based on the proposition that life is so diverse that identity of human behaviour is ruled out and any attempt to force it upon an individual or community ends up in a theory of ultimate behaviour. Self-education would have to be condemned to an obscure existence if we insisted on this ultimate behaviour. Self-educating experiencing relies on the assumption that it is possible as experimentation; and if this can be guaranteed, then experimentation will become a second nature to the willing individual and works as a self-motivating force. The degree of experimentation in self-education is higher than in formal education. In self-education we are alone in our responsibility for directing experimentation. We want to profit from it, not someone else, that is why we are ready to undergo the experiment. Without experience and experimentation there would be no self-education. Self-education is a teacher-less but never experience-less education. The truth in self-education does not depart from human nature, it is conditioned by human nature in the sense that only humans are searching for truth. "If what is regarded as truth departs from human nature, it may not be regarded as truth."[65] We may then assume that it is something we do not know.

Second, to be ready for experimentation, is this a conscious state? Does if mean to be ready all the time or only selectively? How far can we be ready when we obviously dislike a situation? To be ready for experimentation in situation truth means to be sure about the commitment to situation truth. If this commitment is weak, we might as well consider not to strive for situation truth. Conscious it is only when the commitment is high and transformed into the conviction that it is good to pursue situation truth even if we do not like a situation. This can then cause only embarrassment but not untruth. The problem with situation truth is that if we are trying to avoid the harshness of it, then we will be going for compromises. As necessary as this sometimes it, as disadvantegeous it is for building-up a consciousness which is devoted to the truth of a situation. The habit of compromising may lead fast to mental laziness, anti-social conscience and corruption. All of them start as self-censorship in our mind.

Third, what is a situation anyway? What about the history of a situation? How far does a situation stretch? Can it be clearly marked? Truly a difficult problem. If we stretch the lasting of a situation too far, then we are in danger to end up with a whole which may have extraordinary powers of persuasion at its command. The longer the situation, the more generalization is needed and granted, and the nearer we are to fixed truth and, later, ultimate truth. The shorter the situation, the more do we notice the threat of being too fleeting in our pursuit of truth. Thus the answer lies somewhere in the middle. The situation should be examined in its historical setting, since we need this historical knowledge in order to be able to de-socialize the concept which is before us. But we can stop when we do not anymore feel the touch of presentness, the connection to something which is elementarily ours. The same maxim should be applied to the historical dimension of a situation: it is necessary to see a situation from as many angles as possible but not at the expense of a focus. There is a limit to the capability of experiencing and experimenting. If we went on to widen the area of a situation in topical or temporal terms, we would again be vulnerable to end up in a holistic mode which is so tempting to be packed with each and everything of a concept in order to make it universally acceptable. But this is not necessary, truth is not a matter of numbers and it may be embarrassing at times to others. We are not searching for situation truth in order to be liked; rather we are committed to it because it promises goodness in life.

Was Gandhi's mode of searching for truth a holistic one? It was certainly more than what we understand by interdisciplinary. Gandhi was hardly bothered by the boundaries of academic or practical subjects. He was cautious to admit his ignorance or limited knowledge. Regarding political or educational processes he followed a "cautious empiricism"[66] based on a meticulous examination of the situation in its social context and with a view to its future implications. This he weaved into a whole were his own interest of becoming a good person was never forgotten. That is why it is justified to see in him perhaps one of the few examples in world history "who (though) in spite of the fact that his primary aim was the attainment of a state of consciouness which was undisturbed by anything outside itself, (was) yet engaged in a socio-political activity of the most disturbing kind"[67]. This mix of both, the public and the private depended in its success on a scrupulous self-examination and mental purgation "based upon appeals to conscience and experience"[68]. This appeal Gandhi saw firmly realized by the "empire of thought", in which he considered thought to be infinitely "more powerful than either speech or bodily processes" which to him were "mechanical"[69]. However, the means of thinking could not only be a matter of intellect (nyaya) but also one of the heart (yoga), and only the two together would cultivate desirelessness[70] which is the key to the control of mind and action. But even thought is action[71] and thus necessitates the question of how significant the role of reason is in this task. Gandhi held reason in high esteem and regarded it sometimes as the only "guide" to distinguish between the right and the wrong. But he also used the term "virgin reason"[72] which may point out that not only viewpoints were important for him. Viewpoints are "amenable to rational inquiry" and so are "external knowledge" or "worldly knowledge"[73], he maintained, but only "inner knowledge", i.e., "self-knowledge" would lead to inner purity-and only "faith" could help cultivate this.[74]

Thus, for Gandhi, searching for truth was an activity directed to the two areas of knowledge, the inner and the outer, and was, seen from this angle, holistic.

Experiencing and experimenting lead to a state where we are sure that we can discover new things. But would such a continuous process of discovering not affect a person's mental stability? Surely we cannot go on endlessly with experimentation since we are not able to live a life on the edge for long; we need also the stability of fixed knowledge which is being acquired either in self-study or in other-education. That is why we need both, the learning and teaching of standardized knowledge which we simply believe and the learning in open experiences and experiments. To draw the line between the two has to be done by each person alone according to his capacity and need. It should not often be determined by other people since marking the line between the two is in itself a self-educative experiment. There may be x-number of fluid stages between the two forms, and what is too much to bear for one is just the beginning for another. On the ground of this we could never convincingly argue that self-education is finally a more productive form of education than other-education.

Situation truth is not only a way but also a state. As a state it is a result of something which has induced someone to be moral. What is this 'something'? It is the compulsion to be moral. It is the will to be moral; this will can be found only in rational beings. It is this will which provides human beings with self-determination based on an end. But is this 'something' the central agency for all our moral behaviour? And if so, how can it be explained? In my understanding that this 'something' is indeed the central agency I should like to follow the Kantian explanation that every rational being "exists as an end in himself"[75]; therefore this 'something' must also be regarded as an end and not merely as a means. Without going into a discussion of Kant's argument that God must exist, to regard man as an end in himself is the most important contribution to a humanistic attitude. Man is not someone to be used for a particular purpose, for instance to the satisfaction of a supernatural force, a government, a ruler, a traffic policeman, or any other person even if this person is very close to oneself. I shall use Kant's line of arguments for getting clearer about our proposition that self-education is humanistic.

At the outset is Kant's categorical imperative

which leads to the general imperative duty: "Act as if the maxim of your action were to become by your will a general law of nature."[76] This contains a two-fold instruction. It is asking us first to educate ourselves by taking care of our own actions, and second to educate ourselves by taking care of our responsibility. One's actions shall be directed towards the benefit of oneself as well as towards the benefit of humankind, and one's responsibility shall be guided towards oneself as well as towards the benefit of humankind. This is self-education par excellence in relation to its goal: the individual always in the light of society, the individual never without the social dimension. Duty is at the heart of self-education. And above all: what you want for yourself, do want for humankind, and what you do not want for yourself, do not want for humankind-a perfect cycle of congruence.

Kant deepens the argument by asserting that autonomy of the will is the supreme principle of morality.[77] Here we have a clear confession to the importance of the individual with which each and everything starts in life. And not only that, but a preference to the thinking being; and once a thinking being, no authority can be easily imposed on him. But this freedom carries responsibility, namely to be moral. Here self-education is challenged never to ignore its social and humane dimension, humane towards oneself and towards others. Thus, autonomy of the will is an undisputed call for congruence.

Autonomy of the will is explained, above all through the concept of freedom.[78] Freedom guarantees autonomy of the will, and in turn autonomy of the will depends upon freedom. Freedom means to utilize all one's faculties to be able to practise autonomy of the will. It includes the necessity not to exercise too much of self-restraint when critical situations demand one's standpoint and action. Freedom is too easily curbed by threats of sanction. Self-education is to prove itself in those situations when compromise is often the way out for many. Self-education, then, has to overcome reluctance: it is rooted in freedom as the key explanation to the autonomy of the will. This freedom is opening the way to truth via sovereign knowledge, the instruments for a congruent connexion between thought-content and action.

Kant then assumes that this concept of freedom as a quality of the will must be ascribed to all rational beings.[79] This is indeed an idealistic proposition which has been proven wrong throughout the history of humankind. But here the pedagogue in Kant took over: the will to believe that something that is good for me or that is considered by me to be good for others must be considered good by these others as well. Freedom has to be gained through self-education by the individual for himself. In the end the number of single persons following the maxim of freedom by their own decision is more important than a number of people who are told to be free. Self-education, taken seriously as an alternative and complementary form of education, may have a chance to support this process making the individual free. Self-education is not an all-or-nothing affair, there are many degrees to which a practice or a system can be different at any given instant.

How far do we now in self-education work with phenomena and how often do we claim to address the things-in-themselves? Kant recognizes the "inner sense" and the "ego"[80] as forces which can play havoc with our objective will and reasoning. And surely these two have done so all the time. The vague inner sense and the interest-bound ego are powers to reckon with. They can prevent the attempt to educate oneself by simply refusing to undergo the process of self-mastery which is lifelong; and the ego would act as a guide so that nothing bad could happen – it would function as a protective cover. Why to go through an ordeal of educating oneself when such convenient means as the inner sense and the ego are available and would always act in the interest of oneself!

And let us not be mistaken about one thing. Not many people want more from life than precisely this. We are able to go beyond this attitude only when we are not "begging a principle" (of morality) but indeed conceive ourselves as free and through this "transfer ourselves into the world of the intellect and recognize the autonomy of the will with its consequence, morality"[81]. Recognizing consequences is self-education, it is the beginning of joining in the practice of congruence.

Finally, Kant concludes that the categorical imperative is possible because one is made a member of the comprehensible world through the concept of freedom, whereby all one's actions would always conform to the autonomy of the will. Here we have to struggle with the well-known problem of 'is' and 'ought' which, by Kant, was solved by declaring the categorical 'ought' "a synthetic a priori position in so far as there is added to my will, as affected by sensible desires, the idea of the same will belonging to the world of the intellect, pure and practical in itself".[82] We know that this does not work: there is no pure and practical consequence as congruence.

If it is pure, then 'is' would be identical with 'ought' and could not be practised; if it is practical, the 'ought' is different from the 'is' and is not pure any more.

Gandhi reflected at length on this age-old dilemma of means and ends which is at the moral base of the problem of 'is' and 'ought'. There is his categorical dictum explained time and again in various situations, that the ends never justify the means.[83] He never waivered on this fundamental principle carrying it through his whole active life as a banner. It enabled him to state that a seeker of truth would say: "I will be what I ought to be"[84]. The crucial thing for both, Gandhi and Kant, was to get people "to do what they know they ought to do", not to teach them what is right and wrong[85]. This demonstrates a confidence that is amazing given that the problem belongs to those philosophical questions which have occupied thinkers over millenia.

Gandhi's solution to the problem was "to adapt a means which was in a sense itself the end"[86], in other words, he declared means and ends as "convertible terms"[87] with satyagraha as non-violent striving after truth being the means as an "end in the making"[88]. Such an approach, according to Gandhi, would never fail; it would not deny contradictions and compromises but it would highlight the choices one had to make, but not beyond one's conscience. If not very logical, his reasoning was of an immense practical nature, for it appealed to any person to become moral. A concentration on the means[89] is focussing on 'becoming' which in turn denotes the inherent pedagogical process in man.

But this inherent pedagogy of ends and means exists only in the mind of a person before and during an action. Ends can be goals or results (consequences) but there is no causal connection between means and goals, however there is one between means and results; this connection would be ascertainable through inductive logic.[90] On the other hand, only through empirical investigation could we discover whether a particular goal in a given situation would coincide with the result of a particular means.[91] This was the position Gandhi felt he had to master all the time. He searched for a solution in ahimsa as the only means for the realization of truth and accepted it as the ideal of supreme duty[92] which compelled him to be moral, i.e., truthful. Gandhi used 'truth' as an end in two senses, first as "the final ontological Reality (or God)" and second as "our oneness in spirit".[93] The truth in the second sense "as the perception of our essential identity is almost the same as ahimsa".[94] Thus, the mastering of this pedagogy is like the mastering of stamping the two sides of a coin. It means to be free from all dependence. However, this perfect independence from all mundane matters is unattainable otherwise we would not strive for it. Here again we have Gandhi as the educator who knows that impure means result in impure ends[95], and that this is a temptation any educator has to solve first for himself before he tries to transform it to an audience. 'To solve' here means testing, experimenting, experiencing, but always in terms of ahimsa[96]. It also means that it has to become part of one's life and must not be considered as a "mere experiment"[97]. But the distinction between ends and means is not always false and useless; it becomes misleading and dangerous only when we dogmatize that there is a fixed hierarchy of goodness or a single supreme good.[98] The Pedagogy of means and ends becomes so embodied in a law of life. Self-education is consequently a constant challenge to the social and economic conditions in man's life. Self-education can help man create himself in his real earthly life.[99]

To follow the principle of congruence means to act in a given situation in accordance with newly found facts of truth which can make man gradually become aware of his potential and limitations and is thus building upon a healthy foundation of scepticism a robust and down-to earth estimation of himself and his surroundings. It is to make man aware of his own situation in life, his reality. To pursue this strategy means to apply the same moral label consistently to everything which fits the description of what is judged as right or wrong.

Freedom and autonomy of the will are dependent of each other through a congruent connexion, freedom determining thought-content and autonomy of the will enforcing action. Freedom is the over-riding thought-content,autonomy of the will the base for any action. In other words: If freedom is considered to be the thought-content upon which all other thought-content is built, then it is also the condition for the creation of sovereign knowledge. For building up sovereign knowledge a condition is needed which enables man to create it, from another pole, and this is man's will to do so. That is why we can argue from this graph

←freedom → sovereign knowledge ←autonomy
of the will → (truth)

that we have a cycle in which each element is of equal importance. Whether or not we call sovereign knowledge 'truth' is not important as long as we preclude the possibility of absolute truth from our scheme. Sovereign knowledge would be related to relative truth or situation truth. And this is as hard a labour as perhaps to immerse oneself in mysticism or ecstacy which is the road for some to achieve absolute knowledge or truth or the search for a formula that could deliver all truth and harmony.[100]

The rationale behind this is to establish reason for our acts of choosing and deciding. They are based in a given situation on the practice to act in accordance with newly found facts of truth. For this, we need a mental relation to the former and a social relation to the latter. The reasons which finally may appeal to us are of a relatively small number, all of which show much interconnection and mutual kinship. Here congruence is to know something which is to become relationally identified with an existent entity as it is. To know a tree is not to be a tree but it is the capability of the mind to be relationally one, not physically.

Let us now consider the self-educative potential and limitations of such a congruent, that is humanistic, action. While so doing, we should be able to get clearer about the equation of congruent and humanistic. Thus, we can shed more light on our hypothesis that self-education is humanistic in which case it could be replaced by the proposition that self-education is congruent.

A congruent action, or the attempt to achieve congruence, demarcates the potential from the, limitation. We do know soon whether we live up to our expectations when we are educating ourselves seriously or not. The moral pressure[101] which is exerted on us by ourselves in self-education can either produce the best in a situation or be too much and therefore be dropped and therefore cease to be a pressure at all. This moral pressure can hardly be reduced in a therapeutic manner; instead, the pressure of being congruent may lead to an either-or situation: either we educate ourselves according to the ideal (= potential) or we leave it at all and capitulate before our limitations. Self-education, so understood, can become a mental prison whose results may be detrimental to its declared objectives. Unreasonable demands would lead to chinks in our armour of self-protection and self-pity.

Any of these consequences would be found in the interpretation of self-education as a means to an end. As a means, self-education would be judged whether it is successful or not, and success would be generally measured whether a consequence would suit us in a situation or not. As such, self-education would be exclusively product-oriented. But ends and means are so entangled with each other that if you change one you also change the other; the stability of the means-end relationship is needed to succeed in action.[102] That is why being an end in itself, self-education would be a process of steps realizing itself without the pressure of goals for each and every step. Without this pressure a congruent connexion is much more sustainable through an estimation of oneself, whether we are strong enough to have the ideal always before us, or whether we allow ourselves breaks from congruence. This means that we have to know ourselves or, better, that we have to employ self-education and its main principle of congruence in order to learn to know ourselves. It will be difficult to enforce the first, whereas the latter seems to be more pragmatic and attainable. Here a healthy scepticism and a down-to earth evaluation of ourselves is needed in order not to be overwhelmed by self-educative pulls and their peristence with congruence. Congruence with a humane touch means to follow a principle which is desirable in its outlook but not totalitarian in its practice. We need the freedom of choice even for obeying or rejecting congruence. If this is not granted, then we undermine the connection of the concept with situation truth. There may be a situation truth which resolves in the rejection of being congruent. To admit this could not be damaging but would finally contribute to our growth as educational beings. We would be able to rely on us and our ability to care for ourselves (not only to educate ourselves) and would thereby follow one of the major goals of humanism. While loosening the grip on ourselves we are also more willing to accept the individuality of the other. What a sterile communication would we have, if everyone followed the principle of congruence! In such a case, self-education would be redundant and we would be soon on the lookout for a substitute, eventually searching for absolutes. The categorical imperative is not a problem from the point of its content, but certainly one from the point of its form as an imperative. It may be an imperative that covers as much as possible of the well-being of all, but that this has to be done by an imperative is precisely the problem. Autonomy of the will is in principle limited through any form of an imperative. The rational being who wants to unfold his potential in a life determined by freedom, sovereign knowledge and the realization of a situation (truth) will be able to live up to this only when there is a margin for leaning back, pausing and reflecting on the validity of any imperative or any essential. In sum, we would be well advised to allow our principle to become a situation truth which then is relative and fragmentary. This may seem to be a guarantee for a humanistic form of communication. Anyhow, the consequences of an action would make us aware of the impossibility of an absolute self-education or congruence, but it would be more in line with the maxim of acting with foresight, namely not to indulge in absoluteness because each step further into this direction would usher us more into the realm of the belief in a supernatural force and thereby away from our own responsibility.

The temptation to jump unto the search for absolutes is great because those things which are unknown to man could then be explained away. To avoid this is possible. To begin with, we have to understand the temptation and assess whether we are vulnerable to it or not. If not, so far so good; if yes, we ought to counsel ourselves into a situation truth which would reveal also our motifs and beliefs for the moment. Through this we are perhaps able to conceive of this as a truth which is only ours at a particular time and therefore independent of someone or something else. Thus, even a situation truth of a belief in a supernatural force and the absolute would be a humanistic attribute since we would know why we were in need of it at a particular time. We would be in a situation where we would have to understand that nothing could save us from ourselves and that there is only the "universe of human subjectivity"[103]. We may even go further in our conclusion and assert that our will to know our own individual selves knows no limit and that, by this, selves may be relegated to the status of means, but that they as means are the guidelines for a process of progressive self-interpretation as the centre piece of any humanistic education .

4. Self-Educating Experiencing and Congruence-Yielding

In self-educating experiencing man is guided not so much by new factual knowledge but by the humanistic quest to acquire new perceptions whenever a context deems it necessary. This occurs usually in times of crises and perplexity. Meaning is then given to the thought-concept by referring it to the reality of man's experience.

What kind of knowledge are we trying to achieve in self-educating experiencing? It is not the knowledge which only adds to the routines like eating the right things and having enough sleep. This knowledge belongs to a group of actions which we have to exercise in order to sustain life. If we discontinued them, we would die. Since nobody wants this in normal life, we are tending to do routine things instinctively right. It is not the knowledge either which is forced down our throats through a dead school curriculm which is hardly ever related to the life of pupils. And if we restrict our understanding of self-education to self-study, then any knowledge which we want to pick up intentionally could be our object. It may be a craft we want to learn on our own or a course in speculation on the stock-market. In either case we would pursue the matter as long as necessary or as long as our interest and persistence lasted. Once we have acquired this kind of knowldege or lost interest in it, self-education as self-study has fulfilled its purpose and we turn away from it. The knowledge we have obtained is knowledge for a particular purpose, generally highly applicable and meeting short-term needs. Acquisition of knowledge for a particular purpose is closely linked to our capacity to be self-disciplined for a limited span of time. The more help we can get from outside for this, for example from a teacher or a specially designed material or an appropriate media programme, the more successful our self-study is bound to be. But even this is not the knowledge we have in mind when we consider the education of oneself and not the study for oneself. Here our autonomy of choice is determined by an achievement and is not so much a condition as a basic criterion of an educational achievement.[1]

But let us consider again the example of self-study of, say, computer skills. As said above, the actual self-learning of these skills belongs to self-study which ceases to be an 'active' act, that is it ceases to be a condition, as soon as the task has been accomplished. However, once we have asked the question why we have attempted to learn these computer skills and why we have learned them in self-study, we might be able to shed light on the nature of self-educative experiencing as well. The answer lies in the way how we are taking over responsibility for ourselves.[2]

We have probably felt a need to acquire computer skills because we need them to secure a job-this need has determined our want. Eventually there was the alternative of learning these skills and getting the job or not learning them and not getting the job. And since time was not available for a regular course, or a training institute was not around the corner, we tried our luck by way of a self-study programme in order to make us knowledgeable as fast as possible.While doing so we were very resourceful and probably found a number of aids which helped us learn. In such a scenario we have reacted to a situation of crisis in which we had to decide between the either or the or, in other words, our action was based on choosing and deciding in an either-or situation. Once the decision was taken, we found the best possible way to put our intention into practice. This was primarily done not to self-educate ourselves but to achieve a practical goal, namely to be competitive for a job we were interested in. But it also includes a self-educating experience though it may be at first sight only a side product which we sometimes realize only later or not at all. The experience was that we were able to help ourselves in regard to a desire. If we have gained this experience more than once, we will gain more confidence in looking for solutions within ourselves and will refer to them in future more often and more consciously.We can finally rely on this self-educating mechanism whenever it is needed. Looking back on such an experience we would know that, on the way, we had had to choose between two alternatives and to decide on various ways of implementing this choice. In sum, in a situation of crisis we tend to refer to experiences we have either made earlier or which, if new, do promise us relief from our problems. This experiencing is not so much related to knowledge which is factual, rather it is the gaining of new perceptions, in our example the perception of being able to learn something of which we had no idea earlier and to be able to rely on ourselves for this and not only on others. This seems to be what Kant pointed out as an experience being the "occasion for our coming to know something without its being the case that we get the knowledge from experience".[3]

This perceptual knowledge forms the bulk of knowledge in self-education. It is knowledge which has always something to do with us as a person and is thus never fully neutral or objective. It is knowledge which results from the world of man and his relationships and from his creative desire for self-expression. We are part of this knowledge, that is why it cannot easily be transmitted to others; it can be communicated but not under the pretext that it is a blueprint for others. It does not work as an advice but only when it has been experienced. It is created not only in times of crisis but also in times of perplexity, i.e., when we are genuinely confused. Self-education puts us into a position where we are stimulated to find a way out, a way of reducing or eliminating this state of perplexity by drawing upon self-educating experiencing. This we can do on a systematic basis while taking into account earlier experiences and being ready to experimet with new things. One main characteristics of self-education is that it is open in content and methods (this does not, however, supersede the principle of congruence). Crises and perplexities become so less threatening and though not every self-educating experience is a perfect solution to a problem at hand, knowing that he can be self-reliant does a lot to convince man that he can earn knowledge for self-realization whenever needed.

Knowledge gained in self-educating experiencing is first and foremost evaluated by the agent himself and only in second place by an outside agency. In the latter case it is usually an indirect assessment (e.g. getting the job or not in our example above). In case of self-evaluation we are faced with another chance of self-educating experiencing since evaluation as such is ideally always searching for truth. So we have two kinds of experiencing, the one which is experiencing the nature of knowledge, that is relief from crisis and perplexity, and the other which is evaluating this experiencing. If this kind of self-education appears to be an arbitrary and somewhat inconsistent one, then this view might carry some justification. Self-education is not a well-demarcated activity, it is not a science which can be systematically planned (though the experimentation phase, if there is any worth its name, can be very systematic), it is not time-bound or restricted to a particular location (as we have in formal or other education). Self-education is often sporadic in its 'peak hours', then when a person is facing a crisis or a complex situation, but as a basic attitude which can be activated any time it is always there: a kind of latent, dormant self-education potential. The basic attitude is the will to strive for a congruent connexion between thought-content and action. And if this attitude is unblemished by vested interests against freedom, knowlegde and truth, then it is a perfect means for the end self-education. But we may also see it the other way round: Self-educating experiencing as a means adding continually to the end 'congruent action' which is (the same as) self-education. Not that this cycle is a self-contained process, because there are factors which can put it off the rails very fast, for instance a reward which is promised by other means which are to be gained more easily and which are more profitable. Temptations like these are around in abundance, and nobody should claim that he is above them. We like to fall for them—and should even do so provided they finally prompt us to more or new reflections on our involvement in them. Thus they would enrich our self-educative potential.

But undoubtedly, the concept of self-education is the vehicle for humanistic attributes. Above all, it accepts the consequences of an action in such a way that there is no easy resort to a final cause or a supernatural power which would direct and explain. On the contrary: If we find ourselves guilty of improper means, we ought, consequently, try to discover the reason for this in us and should not be surprised that the end we have aspired for has eluded us. It was our 'free will' to choose the means. Experiencing has then become 'trying' as an active means and overcome a more passive form of experiencing which would be 'undergoing'[4]

The knowingness which helps create situation truth is gained through congruence-yielding which is a form of knowing that is either a manifestation of a desire springing from knowledge or an extra-cognitive desire which impels man to know.

Self-education is knowingness. It is knowingness of our ability (or inability) to educate ourselves; further it is the knowingness of the boundaries of self-education, how much we can expect from it and how far we can go with it; it is also the knowingness of (the means for) situation truth. Here we focus now on the latter and its creating situation truth through congruence-yielding.

Let us first consider knowledge creation as a manifestation of a desire springing from knowledge. To create knowledge which is a requisite for congruent thought-content and action may have a moral impetus or root. We want to be congruent because we consider this an obligation, a duty. By this we are induced to create knowledge which can build the bridge between thought-content and action. As such, this is not worthless but built on sand because the morality, that is the sand, can shift and so its focus on knowledge creation. Instead of stressing the moral motif for congruence-yielding, we should prefer to speak of a desire (contrary to Kant) as an empirical condition for further knowledge and congruent knowledge.

Since there is no chance to reach the end of knowledge and knowledge creation because there will always be an unknown, the desire to know a fraction more of the present unknown seems to be a legitimate wish and need not be limited to any formal education. Everyone, given the opportunity, wants to extend his knowledge which is always building on something we already know. It is not so much the act of conquering which propels us to know but the desire to understand. But this need not be an explanation of the desire that to know is followed by a congruent action or is even congruence. How can we come to this conclusion though we are rarely achieving this result in practice? Maybe it has something to do with our desire for systemacy in the sense that for us learning or creating knowledge is simply an event of (also) relating[5]. Whatever we pick up consciously, we relate to something we already know. This is even so in knowledge that we pick up rather casually and without a clear purpose. As we relate pen to paper or paper to writing, so do we relate any new knowledge to prior knowledge. There seems to be no way of creating knowledge without relating. This relating is finally yielding congruence when it has become part of an 'internal curriculum'. We can explain this as follows.

Action presupposes a conscious being[6], more so an action which is conceived as a congruent action, that is an action which is executing a thought-content with as much closeness to its intention as possible. Here we have not only the mechanic action or the typical action with more than a reflex or clear-cut intention, but also an action with a curriculum, an action which intends to bring about a consequence[7]. This curriculum is being bestowed on action by oneself. What is now the difference between the intention and the curriculum of an action? This difference is found in the expectation of what an action should achieve. An intentional action is looking for an experience which might be possible, an experience that is not certain to be gained at the outset of the intention. The action which is following such an intention is the probing into the possibility and is resulting in an either affirmative or negative answer; in the latter's case the intention may have to be changed. In case of an action with a curriculum we are following a course that has been designed according to an imperative: for example to follow the principle of congruence. The consequences of thought-content and action involved in this process are of secondary importance inasmuch as following the duty of congruence-yielding can only conclude in ends which are appropriate to the execution of the means (the duty). We are speaking then of a continuum of ends and means in which the fluidity of the boundaries of ends and means is not anymore a problem and in which the selfish has to withdraw. The purity of duty (universal laws) related to the humanistic postulates of freedom, knowledge and truth[8] ought to be sufficient to avoid suffering for oneself as well as suffering fflicted to others.[9] Knowledge is embracing the knowingness of the certainty that the congruence of thought-content and action amounts to situation truth as long as the self in us is truthful to its duty to choose and to decide, so act, and to denote that the supposed man-nature antithesis is false. However, tension will always be there and has to be accepted as the price for congruence.

If, on the other hand, we accept an extra cognitive desire to know, then we do not subscribe to the theory of relating in learning and knowing and will not be able to educate ourselves as explained throughout this inquiry, This is so because extra-cognitive desire is part of metaphysics and theology where the self which is being addressed is not the empirical but something like the formless, the immutable, the immaterial and the absolute 'true' self. In contrast to this, the self in self-education as being represented here is the empirical self. That is why for us the self-as-subject' and the 'self-as-object' belong to the world as objective entities in which the 'to be' need not be mystified into 'being' but in which becoming and belonging are consequently the essence of being.[10] This is not to deny others their belief in the formless self, but since I do not find it helpful for a clarification of self-education, I ignore it for our discussion.

Cognitive desire to know is the humanistic ingredient of self-education. To see us as rational human beings and to know that there is one rationality common to all human beings[11] is a realization which has to be earned through the experience of reasoning which is the single most important means for the end self education. The aim of it is to form a spiritually free individual.[12]

Congruence-yielding is self-educating experiencing. As that it is continually preparing the ground for a development of sources of morality through successive approximations to truth.

Congruence-yielding is an action to establish a conformity between thought-content and action as closely as possible. As such, congruence-yielding is an intended action on which we have decided after having it chosen for a purpose. In other words, congruence-yielding is a conscious action, that what is called a typical action. By this, congruence-yielding is a means for fulfilling a purpose or achieving an end: the purpose being to bring thought-content and action as closely together as possible so that we have a state of near-congruence; the end being to experience this state of near-congruence. In either case it is an action which is ascribed to responsibility. Once we have decided to act in order to achieve congruence, we have accepted the responsibility of this action and are accountable to it. This does not mean that a conscious action has always to be successful; as any intended action it is being executed because the agent believes in its value, but belief is no guarantee for success. There may be the will to generate congruence, but the end may not be congruence. This experience of a 'negative' result and of a failing to realize the end is as well an experience as a 'positive' result. Preconditions for this would be a) to rectify the congruence-yielding, or b) to go back on the (sequence of) thought-content, or c) to understand congruence diffferently. While so doing, i.e., while experiencing one of these three actions, consciousness becomes more and more a mark of congruence-yielding. Thus, a rational being who is striving towards an increase in self-knowledge is a conscious (rational) being who is distinguished from other beings through the inclusion of volition in his experiencing.

Congruence-yielding is the major relation between thought-content and action; as that it is determined by self-educating experiencing. This experiencing is involving the notion of freedom, both of choice (and decision) and action. We are likely to act responsibly when we know that there is the freedom to choose and also the freedom to face the consequences in such a manner that we can be truthful to ourselves. If the action 'congruence-yielding' can lead to this or that result, then we know that we are responsible for the result a and b, and if we are ready to draw a conclusion and put it into practice, then we are willing to learn. This learning is then based on a self-chosen action according to a particular thought-content; it is a composite of the major relation between thought-content and the action belonging to it.

To yield congruence is first of all to will, second to experience, and third to learn by accepting the result (end) or changing it. Both these reactions to a result share a common feature: they are reflexive of what has been done; on the other hand, they do not suffice in ignorance or indifference; they allow something to happen. This happening in congruence yielding is experiencing which becomes self-educating once we have recognized it as a source of learning. Hence self-educating experiencing is determined congruence-yielding whereas congruence-yielding enables self-educating experiencing to happen.

To argue for congruence-yielding may be the will to act in a like manner in order to produce this manner. This is not a causal explanation which would need a law or a law-like statement to govern this action. A full explanation would have to look into motivation, interests, likes, dislikes, desires, etc. This seems not necessary at this place since all these attitudes belong to the human being as a social being, and this would mean that we were lost in meanings which change with each person and social community. These meanings may be of concern for the performer and his community only, whereas we are more concerned with the forms of an interpersonal world. Moreover, these meanings play their crucial part while de-socializing a concept.

Since congruence-yielding is preparing the ground for a steady development of sources of morality through successive approximations to truth, it becomes the yardstick for a good life. But how is congruence-yielding related to sources of morality for universalisable prescriptions? It is not related to traditional sources of morality like family norms, the preaching of religions, or the political leaders' code of conduct for their followers. This would mean that congruence-yielding would be related to a specific content of a particular source of morality. These empirical contents would lead us consequently to a dictatorship of morals and an extreme relativism. By extreme relativism we mean the dominance of.

morals determined by content only and not by content and form. It also means that two values are incommensurate when they cannot be measured by some single yardstick and no meaning can be attributed to the idea of choice between them. Congruence-yielding is more a form than a content, adopting the right means to the ends we have. It is the will which is good "not because of what it performs or effects, not by its aptness for the attainment of some produced end, but simply by virtue of volition"[13]. That is, congruence-yielding is good in itself, and what is good in itself is also good for a good life. But there is a condition to which congruence-yielding has to surrender, and that is its adherence to truth, to help create situation truth by bringing thought-content and action as closely together as possible. Thus, congruence-yielding is engaged in coming close to relative truth. With this the means (life) are as important as the ends (relative truth), in fact a means has become a new end or an end in itself. Ultimately, congruence-yielding is the process of self-education while being at the same time a product of self-education.

Goodness or relative truth in educating ourselves has to be built on morality, either derived from tradition, or being realized by intuitive, situational decisions, or by becoming a process of congruence-yielding between thought-content and action. I consider the last of these three possibilities the most suitable form for a rational being to exercise his responsibility and to realize himself as a person without being dependent on irrational thought but engaged in enlightened self-interest. Congruence-yielding as a means and an end is finally self-educating and a product of this self-educating. It is self educating by way of approximating relative truth; and it is a product of self-educating by way of being the good will(ing) of a rational being. As a process it has access to the self-rooted in a human condition, as a product it has to lean on this self and thereby also on other human beings. Self-education as the product of its process is intertwined with education as a product of its process and thus with everything around itself. Self-education must not be understood as an exclusive affair and concern of the esoteric but as a necessity to contribute to the making of man which can only be man in his full capacity of a personal and social being.

Finally, we may reflect on the idea of congruence in Gandhi which is in turn part of his humanism. This elucidation may confirm some of the thoughts mentioned above, on the other hand it may also show the differences between our thoughts and those of Gandhi.

Self-education is a stupendous effort of the will.[14] It is something between the Kantian 'willing' and the Gandhian 'self-discipline'. Maybe what Gandhi called the "perfectly controlled" thought is somewhat near to what we call the conguence between thought-content and action; it is at least potentially rich in leading to congruence. Gandhi makes this clear by describing controlled thought as a "power of highest potency" which "can become self-acting"[15] Self-education is then self-realization.

This self-realization consists of three steps: first the practice of self-learning, second the production of useful knowledge and third the development of a congruent attitude.

Gandhi understood by self-learning to become constantly better "under effort and discipline", and he saw no "limiting the capacity for improving"; he imagined that he would lose interest in life if he felt that he could not attain perfection.[16] On this way to perfection many impediments had to be overcome. Gandhi put a lot of emphasis on realizing one's own error while trying to become better; he thought that if the mind had once got rid of an error, it would feel light because the cause of wrong thinking had been expelled.[17] Since man is a self-governing being he is prone to commit errors, but also to set them right[18]. For Gandhi, "the right to err and the freedom to experiment constitute(d) the universal and indispensable condition to all progress".[19] It was a point of honour for him to respect criticism and to privilege heresy since he thought that all society today was founded on intolerance.[20] To deal with all this was the task of self-learning.

And as so often in his life, he formulated his clearest ideas while being imprisoned: this self learning is "thirst for knowledge, diligence and self-confidence"[21], and he adds:

"The superstition that no education is possible without a teacher is an obstacle in the path of educational progress. A man's real teacher is himself. And nowadays there are numerous aids available for self-education. A diligent person can easily acquire knowledge about many things by himself and obtain assistance of a teacher when it is needed. Experience is the biggest of all schools. Quite a number of crafts cannot be learned at school but only in the workshop. Knowledge of these acquired at school is often only parrot-like. Other subjects can be learnt with the help of books."[22]

But this learning of subjects and skills was not the whole of "true education" for Gandhi. It had to be supported and supplemented by the "knowledge of the self" so that a person could become "both a teacher and a pupil".[23] Though Gandhi never underrated practical knowledge which was needed for a livelihood, it was the knowledge that "has come from within" that dictated his actions.[24]

Lack of knowledge was for Gandhi lack of concentration and waste of time.[25] He despised half-knowledge and considered it to be "one of the worst evils" and worse than ignorance and as long as one could not deduce a corollary from a principle, one could be held of having "no knowledge of the principle at all".[26] To familiarize oneself with the facts was a must for him, everything else was laziness.[27] Even sharper criticism was poured on those who desired knowledge for purely utalitarian reasons only. He observed that there should be "no incentive for the acquisition of knowledge" and that "the object with which knowledge is acquired nowadays tends to corrupt it, and therefore the absence of an incentive will be entirely beneficial. Knowledge truly so called is intended for one's salvation, that is to say, service of mankind. Whoever has a desire to render service will certainly try to equip himself with the requisite knowledge, and his knowledge will be an ornament to himself as well as society. Again, when the temptation to amass riches is removed, there will be a change for the better in the curriculum of studies as well as in the methods of education."[28]

And on the possession of knowledge he remarked that one should remember "that non-possession is a principle applicable to thoughts as well as to things. A man who fills his brain with useless knowledge violates that inestimable principle, Thoughts which turn us away from God or do not turn us towards Him are unnecessary possessions and constitute impediments in our way. (...) We are there (the Bhagavad-Gita, XIII) told that humility, amanitvam,....constitute(s) knowledge and that all the rest is ignorance."[29]

Some of the above is certainly very much different from our god-less-explanation throughout this study. But our ways join again with Gandhi's when it comes to the consonance between thought and action, to congruence in truth. He is poignant in his conviction that thought is the "power and the life" behind a non-violent action: "We hardly know that thought is infinitely greater than action or words. When there is corresponsence between thought,word and deed, either is a limitation of the first. And the third is a limitation of the second."[30]

Strength to do a thing would come only when we were conceived of its appropriateness [31], and only a sincere example into which you have put "your whole soul" would "affect the lives of other people around you"[32]. From there it is but natural to find out that Gandhi's self-education was determined by, and generated in turn, the outward as a symptom of the inward.[33]

This congruence of the outward and the inward was for him a recurring theme at various levels: teachers should practise virtues "in their own person"[34] so that students can follow them, individuals should observe moral principles of conduct so that nations can become moral[35].Content generates form-but not till the content, in Gandhi's understanding: "spirit", is changed, "can the form be altered" since it is "merely an expression of the spirit within"[36]. To alter content depends on its means: to make the change potent necessitates, to Gandhi, an adequate means, thus "non-spiritual" means would not be able to successfully influence "spirit"[37]. But there is always his warning that total congruence, or in his words the "fully attained ....ideal", is elusive and that all what he could do was to try ceaselessly "to understand the implications of great ideals"[38]. That is why for Gandhi the development of a congruent attitude was perhaps more important than the final attitude itself. Self-education becomes thus an indispensable means and realizes it self as an end by being practised. The heart of self-education is then the activity to yield congruence, namely to will, to experience, to accept and/or to change.

Remains the question whether Gandhi was a humanist? According to a critic who accused him of an "insatiable love of power"[39] the answer would probably be a clear 'no'. For how can the 'lust for power' go hand in hand with the dictum that "man is the maker of his own destiny" or his understanding of "enlightened anarchy" in which "each person will become his own ruler" without hampering the well-being of his neighbours[40]? Doubtless Gandhi has made the problem of power versus humanism a central issue of his encounter with the world. He posed this as a choice before himself and humanity. And since he "raised the means of non-violence to a principle of universal morality for all human ends", his position has also been labelled as "Radical Personalism"[41]. As a yardstick for control of power he saw an open and a tolerant society in which "free choice is maximized and the use of pressure to enforce social norms is minimized"[42].

Yet a much more popular estimation is to see in Gandhi a spiritual humanist par excellence. Gandhi himself hardly commented on this issue, as he normally shied away from discussions about systems of thought. His' was also understood as "sensitive humanism"[43] or as "radical humanism"[44]. The latter is justified by another author because Gandhi had brought "education to the level of ordinary labourers" and because he had posed the view that education is always an emancipation".[45]

The widest view of Gandhi's humanism is to maintain that for him "the centrality of man permeated the entire canvas from leading from ontology to human concern with the most ordinary needs or of the deepest intellectual and spiritual striving."[46]

I should like to add one more dimension why I think that Gandhi was a humanist, and this dimension is the one of lifelong self-eduction as the continual search for congruence.[47] Once this had become part of his life, he was caught by it as the means for an understanding of the human predicament. The great educator he was, he must have relished the thought that by lifelong self-education he could set a sign that there was nothing like a perfect education. Gandhi's was not so much a humanism in a watertight compartment of definitions, but one with a humane touch embracing the inividuality of man as well as his need for community. He observed throughout his life that our dependence on society would teach us "humility"[48]. Gandhi's process of self-discipline via self-education which included to embrace and transform others "is a way of restoring order to the self and the world".[49]

We can well imagine that Gandhi may have subscribed (also) to a form of humanism which starts from the assumption that though man may not be the originator of life in the final analysis, he is at least the designator of life since he creates ideas on life, nature and cosmos. While doing so, he ėducates himself and creates his world all over again. These ideas are certainly not unaffected by his personal history and environment, neither are they free in the sense that they are conditionless. No idea is non-related, any idea is related, either to empirical or to non-empirical material. We do not know when this cycle has begun, nor do we know when it is going to end. It is this acceptance of the unknown which makes man a humanistic being. In this acceptance he creates a condition of freedom, sovereign knowledge, and the truth of a situation. The major vehicle of this humanism is lifelong self-education.

On account of his epistemological position, Gandhi could well emphaize rational discussion and persuasion as the best ways among his methods of disscourse. They were truly humanistic in nature and were ultimately based on the conviction that the perception of human existence is equal to an understanding of universal well-being. Gandhi's method of discourse had a further dimension of self-education insofar as only a person who had always proved that he complied with the principle of congruence could enthuse people to join in his experience and experiments. This in turn reinforced his belief in the validity of his methods used and tested in self-educating experiences.

5. Conclusion

Self-education can now be divided into two components. There is first the self-educating experiencing which via the principle of congruence is the means to the end 'self-education'. And there is second this self-education which turns into a means while realizing the end 'moral life'.

The principle of congruence is of an impossible standard and can never be put into practice throughout a life. It would mean to lead a perfect life which goes against all what we know about human nature and history. We know that we should strive for morality in which ends never justify the means but we also know that we have to permit ourselves some temporary compromise in attitude and behaviour when in critical moments "larger issues are involved and greater things are at stake"[1]. Though the principle of congruence is an idealistic one in philosophical terms, as educators we know that it has to become a realistic one in order to be helpful for making self-education into an achieveable project.

What can be achieved by probably everyone is the development of a congruent attitude which may be adopted as an underlying idea of life, as in the case of Gandhi who conveyed by precept and example. This can then be left to the individual for the formation of his doctrine. Whatever doctrine would emerge, with the underlying congruent attitude, it would be a positive one in which values would not take a shape directed against humanity. The Gandhian satytagraha, the Kantian imperative, the existentialist conscience of responsibility, or the Confucian golden Rule[2], all of them expressions of a congruent attitude, might guide us in our self-educative project: to have a good subjective intent, based on the intrinstic good of a social form (action), and leading to the extrinsic objective of a good result.

Self-education is humanistic not only because of some specific ends of a good life like wealth, rule of law, and the right to participate in the exercise and control of power, but because of the potential purity of it as a means As a means it contributes to self-knowledge by way of conceptualizing sense data. Actions are then interpretations qua choosing and deciding of these sense data and the concept, one by means of the other.

As a means of self-knowledge, self-education is occupying the top-spot in a hierarchy of means because it wills in freedom and because it is an approximation to situation truth.[3] Willing in freedom means, in the Kantian sense, to learn to will freedom and is, thus, practical reason. To believe in reason does not mean to believe in the perfectibility of man, rather it is supporting human will as one of the causative factors in history.[4] 'In freedom' encompasses two processes: first to be aware of, and second to be capable of doing so, that choice, decision and action are deliberately conducted experiments which provide experience. This freedom of action as our ontic freedom is never sociologically neutral. That is why we can only speak of situation truth and not of absolute truth as the content of our social and political freedom, never of our metaphysical freedom. Such a freedom-freedom as a-matter-of-fact used by man-is humanistic: it is an "ideation...resulting from the awareness of environments"[5]. Once the idea of freedom has been formed, it exists by itself and is ingrained in human life. This is the central feature of an educational humanism which is charactized by its method of "enabling ...freedom through freedom"[6]. We have come to learn to respect it as an end, not solely as a means, and we should accept the autonomy of this idea which helps unfold the potentialities of an individual. Self-education is the vehicle of this process and also, in its execution and realization, its humanistic product. The success of any self educative endeavour is being measured by the actual benefit for the human being who has chosen, decided and acted in a congruent manner.

Finally I should like to place self-education, as so explained in this inquiry, in the system of a general pedagogy. This is done as a help for further thought on the topic. Its humanistic stand cannot place self-education in a traditional set-up of pedagogy which would explain and support the well-defined roles of a superior (teacher) and inferior (student) in knowledge production. Its potential is too radical for this and would only lead to either becoming a tolerated outsider in this system or, worse, a co-opted fig-leaf for some pseudo-progressives. Thus the alternative left is simply to boycott the inclusion of self-education into this pedagogy and to look around where better accomodation promises a more appropriate place. This system could be what is called "Critical Pedagogy", and the form in which self-education could do this is "anti-education".

Critical Pedagogy is signified, amongst others, by efforts to understand "relationships as social constructions with historical antecedent".[7] Its major aim is to research, and to live with, truth which is brought down to historical situations. It is aiming at the knowledge about historically specific struggles for education. This knowledge need not be acquired only in other-education but could also include processes of self-education. "Ultimately, critical pedagogy comes down to practical engagements in educating oneself and others, and acting upon this knowledge in particular social settings."[8] This acting upon could be practised in the "new lived-ideologies of anti-education"[9] in which new forms and new directions for the transmission and assimilation of knowledge would be sought. Anti-education should be interlinked with all aspects of society and generate from these interlinkages new forms and directions. It would not be confined to its own institutions but would work in the existing ones. Like anti-education, self-education would not be a new de-schooling ideology, rather it would want to see itself as a self-perpetuating means to promote less distorted ways of perceiving one's own reality and the reality of others. And while doing so, self-education would have, as any education, a normative function: as an end it will always be measured whether it has supported the independent formation of knowledge and truth and the possibilities of freedom. Self-education would also facilitates the transfer of responsibiligy from the institution to the individual which in turn would guarantee that expectations of hope are not suppressed but kindled into a flame of protest against an unending consumption of instruction. As this, self-education has always also an end other than itself, namely freedom from a schooled society in particular and freedom from an institutionlized life in general.

REFERENCES AND NOTES

1. Introduction

1. J. Needleman, 1983, p. 5. He continues that philosophy has "no other task" and that "anything that calls itself philosophy which does not serve this function is simply not philosophy". He adds that modern man has "strayed so far from philosophy that he no longer even knows what this sort of remembring is" and that the experience of deep memory has vanished from our lives"(p. 4).

2. Though 'remembering' is not as rigorous a method as 'analysis', I nevertheless agree with B. Russell (1989, p. 107-109) that "philosophy is the science of the possible" which advocates that a philosophical proposition must be general

and thereby applicable to everything that exists or may exist and a priori which means that it can be neither proved nor disproved by empirical evidence.

3. In this way I do understand J. Dewey's (1976, p. 328) famous dictum that "philosophy may even be defined as the general theory of education". In the same line do I see A. Flew's (1979, p. 94) putting succinctly philosophy of education not as a "philosophy of" since its "topic is so wide in scope that no branch of philosophy can be excluded as being without some relevant commentary to offer".
4. K. Popper, 1985, p. 200
5. J.A. Hughes, [2]1990, p. 6
6. See e.g. G. Shivarudrappa (1985, p. 74) on Dewey's well-known formula.
7. See e.g. P.Edwards (ed) 1967, Vol. 6, p. 237
8. See e.g. G. Shivarudrappa, 1985, p. 16; G.M. Wingo, 1975, p. 24; and E. Hussain, 1959, p. 13
9. J.K.Mehta, 1985, p. 1
10. C. Wulf, 1982, p. 13
11. Consulting the index volume of the ten volume *The International Encyclopedia of Education* (T. Husen/T.N. Postlethwaite, 1985) we find to our surprise the term "self education" not even mentioned once. Similar terms are listed and written about like self-learning, self-discovery learning and self-directed learning, but the concept of self-education does not appear. This may be an indication of the state of affair. We are dealing with a concept and an area of education which is not recognized as a 'natural'

or 'popular' branch of education. There where we find the term, it is often used in inverted commas (cf. R. Sharma, 1973, pp. 357 & 361) as though it were not real education but at best second-rate, an education which cannot be taken seriously, a kind of education for outsiders and exotics upon which the serious pedagogue has to be suspicious. May be one reason for this attitude is the dominance of other-education, that is the education which is being imparted, given by the mature to the immature, the knower to the learner, the teacher to the pupil. The first is often the person with power in an educational encounter, the second is generally the receiver who is depending on the former. It is but natural that the powerful do not want to discard their power. Why to promote self-education in which the person who wants to educate himself takes over the responsibility for himself! This would diminish the influence of a teacher, etc., and this is not desirable! And what is self-education anyway! It has no institution where it is being administered!

On the other hand, there is a strong trend towards the 'self' in learning from the 1960s to the 1980s as has been shown by S./Rassekh G. Vaideanu (1989, p. 146), namely from learning to learn to learning to self-evaluate, from learning to be to learning to be and to develop, and from learning as much for its own sake as for passing examinations to learning as a means of self-realization and participation. This is a trend which is indeed not new. Throughout the (educational) history of humankind the question of self-development was always in the mind of people, either with an emphasis on the spiritual or the intellectual.

Despite the 'failure' of e.g. *The International Encyclopedia of Education*, there is quite a fair though scattered amount of literature on self-education. Without claiming to know each and everything which has been published, the most important recent titles known to this author are: C.Wulf (1982) who provides five objectives from the standpoint of a critical theory of self-education and ten elements with whose aid the self and the process of self-education can be described; K.Wain (1991) who elaborates that lifelong education is a duty owed to the collective and not only to oneself; C.E. Cuypers (1992) who maintains that education as in principle autonomous self-education is an intellectual illusion and that caring about oneself is a much more favourable view on the structural condition of education: J.S. Brubacher ([3]1962, p.67) with his plea for the self-educated pupil; H.S. Broudy (1965, p.8) who understands good formal education as a guarantee for successful self-education in subsequent years and who argues that even in self-education there is a relation between a teacher and a pupil, "although the distinction is within one person rather than among different personalities" (p. 1) and who considers adult education ideally as self-education (p. 337). Among other authors on the subject, G. Martirani (1984) in the description of a group learning experiment in peace education advocates "community self-education in development" (p.185) whereas A.R. Lacey ([2]1986) lists as one of the possible questions for a philosophy of education whether a teacher is needed in education or not and whether educating oneself can occur deliberately or accidentally (p.60).

Richer, of course, is the recent literature on self-learning and self-instruction - see for example J.M. Schafritz et al (1988, p. 424), D.R. Garrison (1989, p.105), R. Pani (1987, p. 429), S. Rassekh/ G. Vaideanu (1989, p. 168), R.J. Wlodkowski (1989, p. 58), J.E. Adler (1993, p. 223) and also the classic "Learning to be "(Faure et al, 1972, p. 209).

Another group of studies is devoted to self-education as the vehicle to the 'self-made man' of American provenience, see e.g. H. Ehlers (1981, p. 170) and S.A. Rippa ([6]1988, p. 179). Self-education playing a role in the formation of the human personality is being dealt with in M.B. Nitin (1992, pp. 519-520), S. Singh (1987, pp. 180-194), and Vinoba ([3]1985, p.30). Two interesting historical examples of self-education are found in H. Silver (1980, pp. 118-119) on the London Working Men's Association Programme and in A.W.P. Gurugé (1985, p. 578) on individual-centred learning in ancient Buddhist education. Critical comments on self-education as a socio-political phenomenon are found in A Faundez (1987, p. 163) and in W. Leirman (1987, p. 11). Finally, a whole theory of self-education could be worked out in the discussion on hermeneutics which also implies an increase of self-understanding on the part of the subject.

12. D. Macdonell, 1989, p. 80. An excellent example for this thesis is given by K.Kumar (1991, p. 15) when he explains the concept of "walled knowledge" created by the English for the colonial curriculum in India. At the heart of this curriculum "was a vision of the civil society, based on eighteenth century English political

ideas. In England, the vision consisted of a dream of bourgeois individuality, equality and security of property; in the colony it became a programme to train a small minority of property holders in the attitudes and skills of colonial rulers. A key attitude was to look upon the labouring masses as a category set apart by certain features of behaviour and character". See also to this A.R. Kamat (1985, p. 11) who maintains that "in practice, goals, objectives and the structural pattern (of education) are largely influenced by the dominant politico-economic structure and the various powerful groups in society" and not so much by the thinking of philosophers and social reformers.

13. G. Srinivasan, 1987-88, pp. 30-36

14. J.N. Findlay,1961, p. 43

15. As has been clearly argued by G.P. Ramachandra (1994) in relation to Collingwood's philosophy of history.

16. One of the most remarkable indications to the fact that other-education, that is teaching, was not always a pinnacle of educational wisdom is found in Vinoba ([3]1985, p. 58) where he comments that "in all the fourteen languages recognized in the constitution of India there is no verb 'to teach' but only a verb 'to learn.' We have artificially constructed a causative form, as sikhana from sikhna, but there is no root word in our languages corresponding to the English 'teach'. We can learn, we can help others to learn, but we cannot 'teach.' "

17. See to this M.C.D, 'Arcy's (1962, p. 7) argument in a similar vein on 'knowing': "You must already know that knowing is, for otherwise you would

not be seeking to know what it is; and besides you cannot get outside it in order to criticise it."

18. M.N. Roy, 1981 (a) p. 104

19. M.N. Roy, [2]1947, p. 34.

2. Self-Education and Congruence

1. S.P. Gautam, 1983, p. 49

2. P.F. Armstrong, 1989, p. 115. To formulate a "strict hierarchy of values", as E.Fromm (1984, p. 53) advocates, does not make them less ideological. Supreme values for Fromm are: self-activated productive personality, "the capacity of man for transcendence", and to develop his love and his reason (p. 52).

3. J.Sarin/D.Goel, 1985, p. 53

4. D. Pears (1968, pp. 110-111) puts 'deciding' into perscpective while arguing that decisions should not be idolized. "They are not very different from desires, and their effect on the future and the foreknowledge which accompanies them are not magical. There is often only a very slight difference between them favouring a particular project most and deciding on it. It may be only that one dismisses the matter, perhaps merely because there is no more time to consider it. And, if we are impressed by the connection between a decision and the future, at least we ought not be superstitious about it. The announcement of a decision may be a sort of certificate, but the decision itself is not one. There really does not seem to be any reason to reject the view that even in the straight-forward case, where an agent claims to know that he will perform a particular action, his claim, although

it is immediate, is founded on a piece of inductive self-knowledge. Of course he may not be exceptional, and what he claims to know about himself may be merely that his constancy is average. But it could be something more interesting than this, since people vary, and it could be mistaken."

5. R. Prasad, 1989 (a), p. 227.
6. J.-P. Sartre, 1949, p. 32.
7. R. Prasad, 1989 (a), p. 112.
8. J. Raz quoted in S.P. Gautam, 1983, p. 56.
9. R. Mehta, [3]1991, p. 148.
10. L.A. Blum, 1980, p. 169. This "capacity for choice" is related to our aims which are determined by our moral self which is, according to Kant, located in the will (p.192). This has nothing to do with the rather modern and utilitarian theory of rational choice which is normative in the sense that it tells us "what we ought to do in order to achieve our aims as well as possible" (J. Elster, 1986, p.1).
11. J.–P. Sartre, 1949, p. 48.
12. E. Agazzi, 1993, p. 9. Agazzi differentiates between cultural relativity and relativism. Cultural relativity would allow for "full appreciation of what is valid within our cultures" and would also entail "the possibility of an attitude of acceptance and adoption of what is 'alien' but might also become 'ours' ", whereas relativism would lead to a sceptical attitude not only regarding the views of others, but also concerning our own values and principles. See to this also U.T. Place (1991, p. 226) who argues that the naive version of the doctrine of social relativity of truth and knowledge has to be

charged as cultural chauvinism and would obviously be self-defeating.

13. The Oxford English Dictionary, 1989, vol. 20, p. 352.
14. K.C. Bhattacharyya, [2]1983, p. 491.
15. M. Dan-Cohen, 1992, pp. 228-233.
16. I Kant 1982, p. 227 in his "Fundamental Principles of the Metaphysics of Morals". By 'maxim' Kant understands a "subjective principle of action" which "must be distinguished from the objective principle, namely, practical law. The former contains the practical rule set by reason according to the conditions of the subject (often its ignorance or inclinations), so that it is the principle on which the subject acts; but the law is the objective principle valid for every rational being, and it is the principle in which it ought to act that is an imperative." (p. 268).
17. D. Krishna, 1989, p. 184.
18. R. Prasad, 1986 (a), p. 131: "To possess the concept of rationality is to be able to recognize (a) when something is a reason for something else and (b) what are one's conceptual or logical liabilities when he admits or acknowledges that something is a reason for something else."
19. W.G. de Burgh, 1949, p. 1; de Burgh continues that "all advance from plurality to unity, from the parts to the whole, and all judgements of value are referred to the non-rational faculty of imagination". There is more than one argument among R.C. Soloman's (1992, pp. 605-609) conceptions of rationality which demonstrates that the so-called "non-rational imagination" is as much based on reason as a hardcore

analysis, above all his first statement that "Rationality is having reasons" (p. 605.). I suppose that even the most complex system or synthesis is having, at least, the reason to exist.

20. K. Harris, 1979, pp. 138-139
21. Though here again I should like to point to de Burgh's position (1949, p.3) which is mellowing our line of argumentation: "I want to question the claim of reasoning to a monopoly of the field of reason and to show that...they (the logical processes) are empty and sterile when severed from other activities - call them imagination, intuition, faith or what you will - which, as integral to all rational thinking, are entitled to be included within its scope..."
22. R.Rorty, 1989. p. 5
23. D.P. Chattopadhyaya, 1989 (a), p. 14. Chattopadhyaya maintains that what is known as the ontic cannot be completely absorbed in the process of knowing. "To say that the epistemic may be treated as the ontic is not to deny the objective reference of the epistemic. Nor is it purported to affirm the complete assimilability of the ontic within the epistemic." (p.14)
24. M.N. Roy, 1989, p. 46
25. A. Bose, 1987, p. 51
26. This is a state similar to the ancient Ayurveda principle of tridosha which, if in equilibrium, promises excellent health. But vayu, pitta and kapha are never in perfect balance, and so health can at best be only an approximate congruence of the three doshas. See to this Shiv Sharma, 1963, pp. 162-185.
27. See to this e.g. G.R. Malkani, 1982, p.420

28. M.K. Bhadra, 1991, p. 7
29. R. Panikkar, [2]1981, p. 9
30. The following paragraphs are based on B.Pflug, 1993, pp. 6-7
31. Quoted in R. Grossmann, 1984, p. 33. A similar theory is being outlined as regards Ayurveda by this author; see B.Pflug, 1992, pp. 107-108.
32. D. Macdonell, 1989, p. 100
33. W. Leirman, 1987, p. 16; D. Schmidtz, 1994, pp. 227-229
34. R. Prasad, 1989 (a), p.386
35. I do not even accept J. P. Sartre's (1949) understanding of absolute truth from this judgement. Sartre advocates that there cannot be any other truth than "I think, therefore I am" and that this truth is "simple, easily attained and within the reach of everybody" (p. 44). Moreover, he asserts that this truth is not a universality of essence but a "human universality of condition" (p. 46). But on closer scrutiny this does not provide a new argument toward the aspect of neutrality. Even if everyone has it or believes in it, it is not neutral; on the contrary, the more people have it, the less neutral it is, because it would be losing fast its individual manifestation. Neutrality does not go beyond one person.
36. J. Larrain, 1981, p. 104

3. Self-Education and Situation Truth

1. P. Alheit, 1992, p. 188
2. T.K. Mahadevan 1975, p. 357 and T.K. Mahadevan, 1973, p. 202
3. D.C. Mathur, 1981, p. 20

4. N.C. Chaudhuri, 1987, pp. 43 & 49
5. A. Jha, [2]1989, pp. 120 & 123
6. M. Gupta, 1982, p V
7. See to this W. Cenkner, 1976, p. 77
8. This inquiry is not dealing with details of all these experiments since our topic is mainly one of structure and not of content. Maybe surprising for some, but it is not concerned with Gandhi's experimentation in the field of education either, though an inquiry in self-education could be the place to do so. But again, describing the educational experiments in the Phoenix Settlement and on Tolstoy Farm (in South Africa) and in the Satyagraha Ashram, at Champaran, and at Sevagram (in India) (see to these M. Thomson, 1993, pp. 78-86. 105-106, 156-164, 235-250, who calls Gandhi's ashrams 'workshops' and 'human laboratories', pp.109 & 165) would lead us away from the structure of self-education.

   Though, on the other hand, there should be a word on Gandhi's ideas of education just to demonstrate that to discuss self-education within these ideas would demand a different inquiry.

   Gandhi's educational thought can be interpreted from different angles:

(a) We can identify three areas of education in Gandhi:

   (1.) his ideas on education in general and on the education system in particular; (2.) his work as an educator in education and in public life respectively (see to this e.g. K.G. Saiyidain, 1981, p. 102); and (3.) his deliberately conducted self-educative experiences.

(b.) The usual way to classify Gandhi's educational thought is to describe his ideas as a fusion of idealism, naturalism and pragmatism—in which idealism is the fundamental, and in which naturalism and pragmatism are the contributory (see e.g. M.S. Patel, 1958, p. 260).

(c.) Another way of looking at Gandhi's educational thought would be to look at Gandhi's system of education pivoted on the three issues love, freedom, and creation. "For love he accepted Neill's definition. To love means to be on the side of... By freedom Gandhi implied liberation. By creation, he drew attention to self-expression." (N. Desai, 1975, p.77; see also N.P.Pillai, 1959, p.18)

(d.) To Gandhi, the colonial education system in India "was a violation of Truth which means it was also a violation of the self of the individual and an impediment to self-knowledge." (G.Richards, 1991, p.105)

(e.) "...the fact remains that Gandhi wanted education...to help India move away from the Western concept of progress, towards a different form of development more suited to its needs and more viable, for the world as a whole, than the Western model of development." (K.Kumar, 1989, p. 591)

(f.) Gandhi's Basic Education Scheme "envisaged a terminal system of elementary education for the age-group 6-14 which was relevant for an agrarian country" like India (P.Acharya, 1994, p.28)

Certainly this last point is the most well-known one in the discussion of "Gandhi and education". Basic Education as a reaction to the education introduced by the British and as an embodiment of the non-violent order Gandhi wished to see established (see to this B.Kumarappa's editorial in M.K.Gandhi, 1956, p.v) was his educational legacy though not much of it is practically left in India at the end of the 20th century. A good summary of it is given by D.G. Tendulkar 1961, pp.186-203. The best way of studying Basic Education is, however, to refer to some of Gandhi's articles written and published around the famous Educational Conference at Wardha 22./23.10.1937, for instance "Intellectual Development or Dissipation" (CWMG, vol.65, pp.72-74), "Speech at Tithal" (CWMG, vol.65, pp.233-235), "Criticism Answered" (CWMG, vol.65, pp.447-453), "Questions before Educational Conference" (CWMG, vol.66,pp. 193-195), "Some Criticism Answered" (CWMG, vol.66, pp.238-241), "Speech at Educational Conference-I and II" (CWMG, vol.66, pp.263-267), "A Step Forward" (CWMG, vol.66, pp.279-280) and "Discussion with Educationists" and "Talk with a Friend" (CWMG, vol.66, pp.340-341).

(g.) As a last point, because of its proximity to our own inquiry, may be mentioned Gandhi's attitude towards "self-study": "It is a gross superstition to suppose that knowledge can be obtained only by going to schools and colleges. The world produced brilliant students before schools and colleges came into being. There is nothing so enobling or lasting as self-study. Schools and colleges make most of us merely receptacles for holding the superfluities of knowledge. What is left out and mere husk is taken in. I do not wish to decry schools and colleges as such. They have their use. But we are making altogether too much of them. They are but one of the many means of gaining knowledge." (*Young India*, 25.6.1931, in M.K. Gandhi, 1980, pp.96-97) And a few years earlier: "Pupils should know to discriminate between what should be received and what rejected. It is the duty of the teacher to teach his puplis discrimination. If we go on taking in indiscriminately we would be no better than machines. We are thinking, knowing beings and we must in this period distinguish truth from untruth, sweet from better language, clean from unclean things and so on." (*Young India*, 29.1.1925, in M.K. Gandhi, 1980, p.38) A critic of modern schooling like I. Illich couldn't have formulated these ideas of 'progressive education' more precise.

9. Salamatullah, 1989, p.13; B.R. Nanda, 1985, p. 58
10. M.K. Gandhi, 1947, p.140
11. Reginald Reynolds (*A Quest for Gandhi*, New York: Doubleday, 1952, p.132) quoted in B. Bhattacharya, 1969, p.139
12. M.K. Gandhi in R. Iyer, 1986, vol.1, p. 22
13. M.K. Gandhi in R. Iyer, 1986, vol. 2, pp.166 & 167, 105
14. Ibid., p. 353, p. 278
15. Ibid., p. 435
16. Ibid., p. 584
17. M.K. Gandhi in R. Iyer, 1987, vol. 3, p. 210. And this certainty is the motto of his life as is aptly formulated in the title of his *Autobiography or The story of my experiments with truth* (1991).
18. R. Iyer, Introduction to M.K.Gandhi, 1986, vol. 2, p. 9. How Gandhi went through a process of experimentation can be studied from this

Autobiography, a book which is a deeply puzzling one. The first puzzle is that it has been written at all though there was hardly any tradition of autobiographical writing in India at the time of its publication. Second, Gandhi wrote about his experiments with truth which according to Hindu tradition is questionable since experiments with truth are considered incommunicable; however Gandhi regarded them as public in nature. And third, Gandhi was primarily engaged in moral and political experiments and less concerned with spiritual truth. Moreover, his experiments have only reinforced traditional middle-class Hindu beliefs and not generated new truths (cf. B. Parekh, 1986). The puzzles may be explained by arguing that Gandhi wanted his Autobiography and other writings above all to be seen as educative for others, and to achieve this he thought it fit to reveal how self-educative experiences even those of a rather naive, ordinary and trivial nature had influenced his own life. That is probably why many of his writings have this kind of didactic touch. Very valuable comments on, and studies of, Gandhi's Autobiography are to be found in C.N. Patel, 1981, pp. 69-71; T.K. Mahadevan, 1969, pp. 45-61; S. Hoeber Rudolph/L.J. Rudolph, 1987 pp.15-17; S.L. Malhotra, 1989, pp.495-511; B. Parekh, 1986, pp. 14-30, B. Parekh, 1989 (b), pp.247-266; E.H. Erikson, 1970 (chapter I/1); S.Visvanathan, 1993, pp. 12-15; and B. Bhattacharya, 1969, pp.130-131.

19. M.K. Gandhi in R.Iyer, 1986, vol.1, p.148
20. CWMG, vol. 68, p. 40.
21. M.K. Gandhi in R. Iyer, 1986, vol. 2, p. 566.
22. M.K. Gandhi in R. Iyer, 1986, vol.1, p. 420.

23. B. Chandel, 1989, p. 49.
24. D. Krishna, 1969, pp. 39-40, who distinguishes the concept of freedom in Indian thought from the one in a western understanding which is in relation to action, willing and intention. A good example of the latter, to which we adhere, is found in Kant who argues "that freedom is a will both to itself and to the freedom of others" (quoted in J.-P. Sartre, 1949, p. 52).
25. S.D. Brookfield, 1989, pp.152-153, uses the term 'historicity' for the awareness of people "of how their individual actions are affected by, and located within, past actions, ideas, and developed structures. Those who possess this awareness place their lives, the social structures within which those lives are embedded, and the belief systems informing them in a historical context. People with this outlook understand the present in terms of the past. They view contemporary events as being partially determined by previous events, rather than as a historical happenings."
26. This is according to D. Davidson's (1973, p.140) thesis that "freedom to act is not causal power". And futher,: "If willing is an act distinct from doing, it might be a cause, but the question would then arise when an agent is free to will. If willing is not an act distinct from doing, then it cannot be a cause of doing. The dilemma is not resolved by substituting choosing, deciding, intending or trying for willing...." (p.139).
27. J. Cottingham, 1991, p.799. Instead, the author pleads for a sane "autocentric perspective in ethics" (p. 805).
28. B.R. Nanda in a session discussion in N. Radhakrishnan (ed.), 1992, p. 63.

29. N.C. Chaudhuri, 1987, pp.48 & 440
30. R.Chaudhuri, 1990, p. 50
31. J.D.Sethi, 1990, p. 1148
32. See e.g. M.K.Gandhi in R.Iyer, 1986, vol. 2, pp.114, 345-346
33. J.D. Sethi, 1990, p.1149
34. M.K.Gandhi in R. Iyer, 1986, vol. 2, p. 33
35. M.K.Gandhi in R. Iyer, 1986, vol.1, p. 77
36. M.K.Gandhi in R. Iyer, 1987, vol.3, p. 548
37. Ibid., p. 551
38. M.K.Gandhi in R. Iyer, 1986, vol. 2, p. 626
39. P.Bowes, 1982, p. 6
40. M.K.Gandhi in R. Iyer, 1987, vol. 3, p. 209
41. CWMG, vol.79,p. 240
42. Comprehensive analyses of Gandhi's idea of relative truth are to be found in R.Iyer ([2]1983), M.Chatterjee (1983), R.Roy (1984), B.Parekh (1989 a)
43. G. Richards, 1991, p. 110
44. R.J. Terchek, 1986, p. 311
45. M.K.Gandhi in R. Iyer, 1986 vol.1, p.143
46. M.K. Gandhi in R. Iyer, 1986, vol. 2, p. 23. The passage which leads to this conclusion runs as follows. "I am an *advaitist* and yet I can support *dvaitism* (dualism). The world is changing every moment, and is therefore unreal, it has no permanent existence. But though it is constantly changing it has something about it which persists and it is therefore to that extent real. I have therefore no objection to calling it real and unreal, and thus being called an *anekantavadi* or a *syadvadi*. But my *syadvada* is not the *syadvada* of the learned,

it is peculiarly my own. I cannot engage in a debate with them. It has been my experience that I am always true from my point of view, and am often wrong from the point of view of my honest critics. I know that we are both right from our respective points of view. And this knowledge saves me from attributing motives to my opponents or critics. The seven blind men who gave seven different descriptions of the elephant were all right from their perspective points of view, and wrong from the point of view from one another, and right and wrong from the point of view of the man who knew the elephant. I very much like this doctrine of the manyness of reality. It is this doctrine that has taught me to judge a Mussalman from his own standpoint and a Christian from his. Formerly I used to resent the ignorance of my opponents. Today I can love them because I am gifted with the eye to see myself as others see me and *vice versa.* I want to take the whole world in the embrace of my love." (pp. 22-23)

47. M.K. Gandhi in R. Iyer, 1986, vol.1, p.40

48. E.Fromm in his Introduction to I. Illich, 1978, p.10

49. M.K. Gandhi in R.Iyer, 1986, vol.1, p.86

50. Ibid., p.118

51. M.K. Gandhi in R. Iyer, 1986, vol. 2, pp.110-111. Though an experiment with truth is carried out first of all on oneself, Gandhi's experimenting involved often other people (M.Chatterjee 1983, pp. 58,68). This experimenting sometimes continued "at the expense of trusting friends" for "there come to us moments in life when

about some things we need no proof from without" (M.K. Gandhi in R. Iyer 1986, vol.1, p. 355). He was also certain that consistent attention to self-examination would enhance his moral credibility in order to "*induce others* to make sacrifices on behalf of shared values" (R. Iyer, [2]1983, p. 69).

52. M.K. Gandhi in R. Iyer, 1986, vol. 2, p.126

53. Ibid., pp.155-156

54. Ibid., p.176.

55. M.Chatterjee, 1983, p. 61

56. Tattvartha Sutra, 1994, p.138

57. R.Iyer, [2]1983, p.169

58. M.Chatterjee, 1983, p. 67

59. M.K. Gandhi in R. Iyer, 1986, vol. 2, p. 200

60. R. Iyer, [2]1983, pp.10 & 152

61. Ibid., p. 379

62. M.K.Gandhi in R.Iyer, 1986, vol. 2, p. 492. Here the well-known passage in full: "At the time of writing I never think of what I have said before. My aim is not to be consistent with my previous statements on a given question, but to be consistent with truth as it may present itself to me at a given moment. The result has been that I have grown from truth to truth; I have saved my memory and undue strain; and what is more, whenever I have been obliged to compare my writing even of fifty years ago with the latest, I have discovered no inconsistency between the two. But friends who observe inconsistency will do well to take the meaning that my latest writing may yield unless, of course, they prefer

the old. But before making the choice they should try to see if there is not an underlying and abiding consistency between the two seeming inconsistencies."

63. "The principle of non-contradiction rules out the possibility that, for the same p, both p and not-p be true." (U.T. Place, 1991, p. 271)
64. A.D.P. Kalunsuriya, 1993, p. 108
65. Confucius, 1966, p.110
66. P. Spratt in S.Ray, 1970, p.207
67. D. Krishna, 1969, p.35
68. M.K. Gandhi in R. Iyer, 1987, vol. 3, p.12
69. M.K. Gandhi in R. Iyer, 1986, vol. 2, p.352
70. Ibid., p.234
71. Ibid., p.226
72. M.K. Gandhi in R. Iyer, 1986, vol.1., pp.478-479
73. M.K. Gandhi in R. Iyer, 1986, vol.2, p.31
74. Ibid., p.32
75. I. Kant, 1982, p.176
76. I. Kant, 1977, p.170
77. Ibid., p.187
78. Ibid., p.191
79. Ibid., p.197, p.193
80. Ibid., p.197
81. Ibid., p.198
82. Ibid., p.199
83. See e.g. M.K. Gandhi in R.Iyer, 1986, vol.1, p.445
84. M.K. Gandhi in R.Iyer, 1986, vol.2, p.198
85. R.Iyer, [2]1983, p. 69

86. J.M. Brown, 1990, p. 393
87. M.K. Gandhi in R. Iyer, 1986, vol. 1, p.404 and 1987, vol. 3, p. 219
88. K. Damodaran, 1969, p. 91. An end (like truth) would anyway ever elude us; that is why the means to this end become supremely important (R.Iyer, [2]1983, p. 230)
89. M.K. Gandhi in R.Iyer, 1987, vol. 3, p. 245
90. J. Bandyopadhyaya, 1969, p. 376
91. Ibid., p. 379
92. S. Khanna, 1985, p.39
93. Ibid., p. 41
94. Ibid., p. 42
95. M.K. Gandhi in R.Iyer, 1987, vol.3, p.592
96. M.K. Gandhi in R.Iyer, 1986, vol.2, p.426
97. Ibid., p.320
98. R.Iyer., [2]1983, p.370
99. See to this K. Damodaran, 1969, p.97
100. See to this J.D. Barrow (1991) who concludes that there is no such formula. "No Theory of Everything can ever provide total insight. For, to see through everything, would leave us seeing nothing at all." (p. 210)
101. This moral pressure is inherent in Kant's moral philosophy as is evident from A. MacIntyre's (1981, p. 48) explanation: "...if the rules of morality are rational, they must be the same for all rational beings, in just the way the rules of arithmetic are; and if the rules of morality are *binding* on all rational beings, then the

contingent ability of such beings to carry them out must be unimportant — what is important is their will to carry them out. The project of discovering a rational justification of morality therefore simply is the project of discovering a rational test which will discriminate those maxims which are a genuine expression of the moral law when they determine the will from those maxims which are not such an expression."

102. D.P. Chattopadhyaya, 1989 (a), p.19; see also Y.N. Chopra, 1991, p. 91, who claims "that the supposed discord between ends and means is a totally false opposition" once we have moved "from the engineering view of practical knowledge" to "those human virtues where pleasure is simply irrelevant"; see further N.K. Devaraja, 1988, pp.132-33, who agrees with M.N. Roy that what is called rationality can be understood as an instrument of "perceiving the inter-connections between ends and means".

103. J.-P. Sartre, 1949, p. 55

4. Self-Educating Experiencing and Congruence-Yielding

1. B.Crittenden, 1979, p.105

2. I am not sure whether J.-P. Sartre (1949, p. 29) is right in assuming that being responsible for one's own individuality means to be responsible for all men since we are following an image of man which we believe he ought to be. Doubting this stems from the belief that "an agent is the ultimate authority with regard to his own intentions" and the

consequence therefrom "that we can never infer with certainty a man's intentions" (S.P.Gautam, 1983, p.52). And if intentions are not certain, how can we then infer from them our condition of existence to everyone's condition of existence?

3. in D.W. Hamlyn, 1979, p. 29
4. J. Dewey, 1976, p. 139
5. C. Titmus, 1989, p. 4
6. M.N. Roy, 1984, p. 21
7. S.P. Gautam, 1983, p. 51
8. M.N. Roy, 1989, p.497
9. In formulating these ideas I owe much to the writing of J.Leibowitz (1990, passim), one in particular, which elaborates the commandment to follow the Tora given by God-but to judge it with human reasoning (p.126).
10. M.N. Roy, 1984, p. 45
11. S. Bhattacharyya, 1992, p. 5. The emphasis on reason in humanism is but one (though essential) criterion. There are other principles which can be stressed equally forcefully, for example the belief in the unity of the human race, the emphasis on man's dignity (E. Fromm, 1986, pp.14-15), a sense of beauty and even an instinct for religion (G.C. Lee, 1965, pp. 69-70), not to act according to ego-consciousness, not to be determined by the dread of death or by the desire for personal immortality, and not to be determined "by either aversion or reluctance to bear the cross of disvalue" (S. Singh, 1990, p.137).

12. M.N. Roy, 1981 (b), p. 61

13. I. Kant, 1982, p. 256

14. R. Iyer regards this effort of the will as an essential characteristic of Gandhi: "...by his fidelity to this views, Gandhi demonstrated the liberating and transforming power of any attempt to fuse metaphysics and conduct, theory and practice, *through an enormous effort of the will.*" (Introduction to M.K. Gandhi, 1986, vol.1, p.11;) Gandhi demonstrated this capacity numerous times in his life in areas as diverse as the ascetic observances in his ashrams and his techniques in fighting South African or British injustice. The example which is, however, the most impressive to this author is his studies of books, above all when imprisoned, which has led one of his biographers to the verdict: *"He never read; he studied."* (B.R.Nanda, 1982, p.123;) But this example points also to the (excessive)? purpose-mindedness in Gandhi, and one is perhaps justified to ask: was there ever a time when he 'relaxed', when he lived for the sake of living? See to this also S.K. Saksena (1986, p. 230) who talks about his "unrelaxing inner wakefulness", p.163.

15. M.K. Gandhi, 1947, p. 163

16. M.K. Gandhi in R. Iyer, 1986, vol. 2, pp. 36-37

17. Ibid., p. 197

18. M.K. Gandhi, in R. Iyer, 1986, vol. 2, p.189

19. R. Iyer, [2]1983, p.160

20. Ibid., p.169.
21. M.K. Gandhi in R. Iyer, 1986, vol. 2, p. 612.
22. Ibid., p. 611.
23. Because of its importance here the whole passage: "If the inmates of the Ashram understand this (that every branch of knowledge should have as its goal knowledge of the self), they would see that the Ashram is a great school in which the inmates receive education not for a few hours only but all the time. Every person who lives in the Ashram to attain knowledge of the Self – of Truth – is both a teacher and a pupil. He is a teacher in regard to what he knows, and a pupil in regard to anything about which he needs to learn. If we know more than our neighbour about anything, we should willingly share our knowledge with him, and equally willingly receive from him what he knows more than we do. If we thus regularly exchange knowledge with others, we would not feel the absence of teachers, and education would become a painless and spontaneous process." (M.K. Gandhi in R. Iyer, 1986, vol. 2, pp. 631-632).
24. Ibid., p.196.
25. M.K. Gandhi in R.Iyer, 1987, vol. 3, p. 212.
26. Ibid., p. 594 and 1986, vol.1, pp. 323-324.
27. M.K. Gandhi in R. Iyer, 1987,vol. 3, p. 440.
28. M.K. Gandhi in R. Iyer, 1986, vol. 2, p. 602.
29. M.K. Gandhi in R. Iyer, 1987, vol. 3, p. 475.
30. M.K. Gandhi in R. Iyer, 1986, vol. 2, pp. 357-358.

31. M.K. Gandhi in R. Iyer, 1987, vol. 3, p. 101.
32. M.K. Gandhi in R. Iyer, 1986, vol. 2, p. 367.
33. M.K.Gandhi in R.Iyer, 1986, vol.1, p.408. See also CWMG, vol.36, p.268: "My outward form is I hope an expression of the inward."
34. M.K. Gandhi in R. Iyer, 1986, vol. 1, p. 450.
35. M.K. Gandhi in R. Iyer, 1987, vol. 3, p. 429.
36. M.K. Gandhi in R. Iyer, 1986, vol. 2, p. 313.
37. M.K. Gandhi in R. Iyer, 1987, vol. 3, p. 73.
38. M.K. Gandhi in R. Iyer, 1986, vol. 2, pp. 278-279.
39. N.C. Chaudhuri, 1987, p. 528.
40. M.K.Gandhi in R.Iyer, 1986, vol.1, p.462 and 1987, vol.3, p.602. In the translation of S.Radhakrishnan, Gandhi's reference to the Gita VI.5 is as follows: "Let a man lift himself by himself; let him not degrade himself; for the Self alone is the friend and the Self alone is the enemy of the self." (The Bhagavadgita, 1992, p.189).
41. S. Joshi, 1991, p. 2567.
42. R. Iyer, [2]1983, p. 249.
43. K.G. Saiyidain, [2]1963, p. 232.
44. M. Thomson, 1993, p. 15.
45. M. Chakrabarti, 1992, pp. 140-141.
46. J.D. Sethi, 1990, p. 1161. The author explains that even humanism as relativism "would also be consistent with Gandhi in so much as it holds that truth and reality, which are attainable, are sufficient for man. Gandhi would also agree with the centrist Humanist doctrine that truths are useful and should be related to human progress. And, finally, Gandhi would

subscribe to the Humanist view that claims to infallibility are wrong and, therefore, human relations should be characterized by tolerance and the absence of coercion." (p.1159)

47 If it were not already a famous book-title (H.G.Gadamer, 1975), we could label Gandhi's efforts in lifelong self-education as *Truth and Method*, i.e., his continual search for truth by adopting various methods of inquiry and communication.

48 M.K. Gandhi in R.Iyer, 1987, vol.3, p.228

49 R. Bharucha, 1993, p.79

5. Conclusion

1 M.N. Roy, 1981 (b), p.34

2 To the existentialist conscience of responsibility see J.-P. Sartre (1949, pp.30-31): "...one ought always to ask oneself what would happen if everyone did as one is doing"; and to the Confucian Golden Rule see W.Lai (1993, p.125): " 'Do not do unto others what one would not desire for oneself.' "

3 M.N. Roy, 1981 (b), p.53: "Quest for freedom and search for truth constitute the basic urge for human progress."

4 Ibid., p.54

5 Ibid., p.55

6 C. Menze, 1991, p.87

7 D.W. Livingstone, 1987, p.10. In addition Livingstone demands from educational scholarship in Critical Pedagogy: (1) to identify "discrepancies between dominant versions of reality promulgated in formal institutions and

the lived experiences of subordinate groups in relation to such institutions", (2) "to take the vantage point of the subordinated", (3) to expand a critical dialogue to the entirety of everyday life, (4) to promote "subordinated peoples' own discussion", and (5) "to deal with different levels of abstractions interwoven within the dominant mode of thought".

8 D.W.Livingstone, 1987, p.223

9 K.Harris, 1979, p.187. Anti-education "would be a matter of people talking, acting and working informally among themselves ; discussing their lives, their freedoms, their constraints, their visions and their knowledge of the discovering of the world for themselves through experience and with authorities, and linking up with movements in other areas of society." (p.188)

BIBLIOGRAPHY

This select bibliography contains as accurate as possible all the works which have influenced my way of thinking over the years while working on the thesis of congruence and on Gandhi. Not all of them are quoted in the text and notes. But this does not mean that they are less important. Some of them are even more significant than works quoted since I have used them less for a single argument but for the fullness of their ideas.

Acharya, Poromesh: Universal Elementary Education. Receding Goal. ***Economic and Political Weekly***, 29 (1994) 1&2, pp. 27-30

Adler, Jonathan E.: Indirect Learning and the Aims-Curricula Fallacy. **Journal of Philosophy of Education**, 27 (1993) 2, pp. 223-232

Agazzi, Evandro: The Meaning of Diversity in Philosophical and Religious Traditions. **Journal of**

Indian Council of Philosophical Research, 10 (1993) 3, pp.1-11

Alheit, Peter: The Biographical Approach to Adult Education, in: Wilhelm Mader (ed.): **Adult Education in the Federal Republic of Germany.** Scholarly Approaches and Professional Practice, Vancouver : The University of British Columbia, 1992, pp.186-221

Althusser, Louis: *Essays on Ideology*, London: Verso, 1984

Armstrong, Paul F.: Right for the Wrong Reasons: A Critique of Sociology in Professional Adult Education, in: Barry P. Bright (ed.): **Theory and Practice in the Study of Adult Education.** The Epistemological Debate, London: Routledge, 1989

Avinashilingam, T.S: **Gandhiji's Experiments in Education,** Delhi: Ministry of Education, Government of India, 1960

Balasubramanian, R.Bhattacharyya, Sibajiban (eds.) : **Freedom, Progress and Society**, Delhi: Motilal Banarsidass, 1986

Bandhyopadhyaya, Jayantanuja: **Social and Political Thought of Gandhi,** Bombay: Allied, 1969

Banerjee, K.K. : **Language, Knowledge and Ontology,** New Delhi: Indian Council of Philosophical Research, 1988

Banerjee, Nikunja Vihari: **Concerning Human Understanding.** Essays on the Common-sense Background of Philosophy, London: Allen & Unwin, 1958

Barrow, J.D: **Theories of Everything,** London: Vintage, 1991.

Barua, Archana: Humanism in Gandhi's Secularism. **Gandhi Marg,** 15 (1993) 2, pp. 222-225

Bhadra, Mrinal Kanti: On Mohanty's Conception of Intentionality, in: Daya Krishna/K.L. Sharma (eds.): **The Philosophy of J.N. Mohanty**, New Delhi: Indian Council of Philosophical Research, 1991

Bhagavadgita, The. With an Introductory Eassy, Sanskrit Text, English Translation and Notes by S. Radhakrishnan, Delhi: O.U.P., 1992 ([1]1948)

Bharucha, Rustom: **The Question of Faith,** New Delhi: Orient Longman, 1993

Bhatt, B.R. (e.d.) **Reality, Knowledge and Value**, Delhi Bharatiya Vidhya Prakashan, 1985

Bhattacharya, Bhabani: **Gandhi The Writer** (The Image As It Grew), New Delhi: National Book Trust, 1969

Bhattacharyya, Krishnachandra: **Studies in Philosophy,** vols. 1 & 2 , ed. by Gopinath Bhattacharyya, Delhi: Motilal Banarsidass, [2]1983 ([1]1958)

Bhattacharyya, Sibajiban: Some philosophical problems concerning culture and rationality. **Journal of Indian Council of Philosophical Research,** 9 (1992) 2, pp. 5-24

Blum, Lawrence A.: **Friendship, Altruism and Morality,** London: Routledge & Kegan Paul, 1980

Bose, Amina: **Dimensions of Peace and Nonviolence.** The Gandhian Perspective, Delhi : Gian, 1987

Bourai, H.H.A. **Indian Theory of Education**, Delhi: B.R. Publishing Corporation, 1993

Bowes, Pratima: What is Indian about Indian Philosophy? in : S.S. Rama Rao Pappu/R. Puligandla (eds.): **Indian Philosophy: Past and Future,** Delhi: Motilal Banarsidass, 1982

Brennan, J.M. **The Open-Texture of Moral Concepts**, London: Macmillan, 1977

Brookfield, Stephen D.: The Epistemology of Adult Education in the United States and Great Britain: A Cross-Cultural Analysis, in: Barry P. Bright (ed.): **Theory and Practice in the Study of Adult Education.** The Epistemological Debate, London: Routledge, 1989, pp. 141-173

Broudy, Harry S.: **Building a Philosophy of Education**, New Delhi: Prentice Hall of India, 1965 ([1]1954)

Brown, Judith M.: **Gandhi.** Prisoner of Hope, Delhi: O.U.P., 1990

Brubacher, John S.: **Modern Philosophies of Education**, New York: McGraw Hill, [3]1962 ([1]1939)

Burgh, W.G.de: **The Life of Reason**, London: Macdonald & Evans, 1949

Cenkner, William: **The Hindu Personality in Education.** Tagore, Gandhi, Aurobindo, New Delhi: Manohar, 1976

Chacko, K.C.: Gandhi as a Theistic Humanist. **Gandhi Marg**, 13 (1991) 1, pp.87-93

Chakrabarti, Mohit: **Gandhian Humanism**, New Delhi: Concept, 1992

Chandel, Bhuvan: Ends versus Means: Controversies and Beyond, in: R.Prasad (ed): **Ends and Means in Private and Public Life**, Shimla: Indian Institute of Advanced Study, 1989, pp. 44-52

Chandra, Pratap: **The Hindu Mind**, Simla: Indian Institute of Advanced Study, 1977

Chatterjee, Margaret: **Gandhi's Religious Thought**, London: Macmillan, 1983

Chattopadhyaya, D.P.: Social and Political Philosophy. Some Aspects, in: Krishna Roy/Chhanda Gupta (eds.): **Essays in Social and Political Philosophy**, New Delhi: Indian Council of Philosophical Research, 1989 (a), pp. 3-24

Chattopadhyaya, D.P. : **Knowledge, Freedom and Language.** An Interwoven Fabric of Man, Time and World, Delhi: Motilal Banarsidass, 1989 (b)

Chattopadhyaya, D.P. : Rationality, Transparent, Cultural and Transcendental. **Philosophy East & West**, 52 (1992) 4, pp. 561-579

Chaudhuri, Nirad C. : **Thy Hand, Great Anarch!** India : 1921-1952, London: Chatto & Windus, 1987

Chaudhuri, Rajit: Gandhi and Value Education. **Gandhi Marg**, 16 (1994) 1, pp. 45-53

Chennakesavan, Sarasvati: **Concept of Mind in Indian Philosophy**, Delhi: Motilal Banarsidass, [2]1980 ([1]1960)

Chopra, Y.N.: Means and Ends, in: Ramakant Sinari (ed.): **Concept of Man in Philosophy**, Shimla: Indian Institute of Advanced Study, 1991, pp. 78-92

(Confucius): **The Wisdom of Confucius**, ed. by Lin Yutang, New York: The Modern Library, 1966

Copley, Antony: **Gandhi.** Against the Tide, Calcutta: O.U.P., 1993 ([1]1987)

Cottingham, John: The Ethics of Self-Concern. **Ethics**, 101 (1991) 4, pp. 798-817

Cowen, Tyler: Self-Constraint versus Self-Liberation. **Ethics**, 101 (1991) 2, pp. 360-373

Crittenden, Brian: Autonomy as an aim of education, in Kenneth A. Strike/Kieran Egan (eds.):

Ethics and educational policy, London: Routledge & Kegan Paul, 1979

Cuypers, Stefaan E.: Is Personal Autonomy the First Principle of Education? **Journal of Philosophy of Education**, 26 (1992) 1, pp. 5-17

Damodaran, K.: Ends and Means , in: S.C. Biswas (ed.) : **Gandhi. Theory and Practice.** Social Impact and Contemporary Relevance. Proceedings of a Seminar, Simla: Indian Institute of Advanced Study, 1969

Dan-Cohen, Meir: Conceptions of Choice and Conceptions of Autonomy. **Ethics**, 102 (1992) 2, pp. 221-243

D'Arcy, M.C.: **The Mind and Heart of Love.** Lion and Unicorn. A Study in Eros and Agape, London: Fontana, 1962 ([1]1945)

Davidson, Donald: Fredom to act, in: Ted Honderich (ed.): **Essays on freedom of action**, London: Routledge & Kegan Paul, 1973, pp. 137-156

Desai, Narayan: The Gandhian Approach to Education, in: Paulo Freire: **Education for Liberation**, Bangalore: Ecumenical Christian Centre, [2]1983 ([1]1975), pp. 76-78

Devaraja, N.K. : **Humanism in Indian Thought**, New Delhi: Indus, 1988

Dewey, John: **Democracy and Education.** An Introduction to the Philosophy of Education, New Delhi: Light and Life Publishers, 1976 (first published in the U.S.A in 1916)

Edwards, Paul (ed.): **The Encyclopedia of Philosophy**, 8 vols., New York: Macmillan & The Free Press, 1967

Ehlers, Henry: **Crucial Issues in Education**, New York: Holt, Rinehart and Winston, 1981 ([1]1955)

Elster, Jon (ed.): **Rational Choice**, Oxford: Basil Blackwell, 1986

Erikson, Erik H. : **Gandhi's Truth,** London: Faber and Faber, 1970

Faundez, Antonio: Dialogue Towards Development and the Development of Dialogue in: Walter Leirman/ Jindra Kulich (eds.): **Adult Education and the Challenges of the 1990s,** London: Croom Helm, 1987, pp. 159-169

Faure, Edgar et al : **Learning to be.**: The world of education today and tomorrow, Paris: Unesco, 1972

Findlay, J.N. : **Values and Intentions.** A Study in Value-Theory and Philosophy of Mind, London: Allen & Unwin, 1961

Flew, Antony (ed.) : **A Dictionary of Philosophy**, London: Macmillan 1979

Freire, Paulo: **Pedagogy of the Oppressed,** New York: Seabury, 1970 ([1]1968)

Fromm, Erich: **To have or to be?** Toronto: Bantam, 1982 ([1]1976)

Fromm, Erich: **On Disobedience and other essays,** London: Routledge & Kegan Paul, 1984

Fromm, Erich: **You Shall Be As Gods.** A Radical Interpretation of the Old Testament and Its Tradition, New York: Fawcett Premier, 1986 ([1]1966)

Gadamer, Hans-Georg: **Truth and Method,** London: Sheed and Ward, 1975 ([1]1960)

(Gandhi. M.K.:) **The Collected Works of Mahatma Gandhi**, New Delhi: Ministry of Information and Broadcasting, Government of India, 1958 ff. (Abbreviated as CWMG)

Gandhi.M.K.: **Self-Restraint**:. Self-Indulgence, Ahmedabad: Navajivan, 1947

Gandhi, M.K: **Basic Education,** ed. by Bharatan Kumarappa, Ahmedabad: Navajivan, 1956 ([1]1951)

Gandhi, Mahatma: **All Men are Brothers.** Life and Thoughts of Mahatma Gandhi as Told in his own Words, Compiled and edited by Krishna Kripalani, Ahmedabad: Navajivan, 1960

Gandhi, M.K. **My Views on Education,** ed. by Anand T. Hingorani, Bombay: Bharatiya Vidya Bhavan, 1970

Gandhi, M.K.: **Towards New Education,** ed. by Bharatan Kumarappa, Ahmedabad: Navajivan, 1980 ([1]1953)

Gandhi, M.K.: **An Autobiography or The Story of my experiments with truth,** Ahmedabad: Navajivan, 1991, ([1]1927)

(Gandhi, M.K.): **The Moral and Political Writings of Mahatma Gandhi,** compiled by Raghavan Iyer; vol. 1: Civilization, Politics, and Religion (1986); vol. 2: Truth and Non-Violence (1986); vol. 3: Non-Violent Resistance amd Social Transformaton (1987), Oxford: O.U.P.

Garrison, D.R.: **Understanding Distance Education.** A Framework for the Future, London: Routledge, 1989

Gasché, Rodolphe: **The Tain of Mirror.** Derrida and the Philosophy of Reflection, Cambridge (Mass.): Harvard University Press, 1966.

Gautam, Satya P.: **Reasons for Actions.** A Praxiological Approach to Philosophy of Social Sciences, Delhi: Ajanta, 1983

Grossmann, Reinhardt: **Phenomenology and Existentialism.** An Introduction, London: Routledge & Kegan Paul, 1984

Grunebaum, G.E. von : Islam in a Humanistic Education, in.: J. Stewart-Robinson (ed.): **The Traditional Near East,** Englewood-Cliffs: Prentice Hall, 1966

Gupta, Manmathnath: **Gandhi and His Times,** New Delhi: Lipi Prakashan, 1982

Gurugé, A.W.P. : Buddhist Education, in: Torsten Husen/ T.Neville Postlethwaite (eds.): **The International Encyclopedia of Education,** vol. 1, Oxford: Pergamon, 1985, pp. 574-581

Hamlyn, D.W: **Experience and the growth of understanding,** London: Routledge & Kegan Paul, 1979

Harris, Kevin: **Education and Knowledge: The Structured Misrepresentation of Reality,** London: Routledge & Kegan Paul, 1979

Hay, Stephen N.: Jain Influences on Gandhi's Early Thought, in: Sibnarayan Ray (ed.): **Gandhi, India and the World.** An International Symposium, Bombay: Nachiketa, 1970, pp. 14-23

Henry, Nelson B. (ed.): **Modern Philosophies and Education.** The Fifty Fourth Year Book of the National Society for the Study of Education, Part 1, Chicago: The National Society for the Study of Education, 1956 ([1]1955)

Hoeber Rudolph, Susanne/ Rudolph, Lloyd I.: **Gandhi.** The Traditional Roots of Charisma, Hyderabad: Orient Longman, 1987

Honderich, Ted: One Determinism, in: Ted Honderich (ed.): **Essays on freedom of action,**

London: Routledge & Kegan Paul, 1973, pp. 185-215

Honderich, Ted/ Burnyeat, Myles (eds.): **Philosophy As It Is**, Harmondsworth: Penguin, 1984 ([1]1979)

Hountondji, Paulin J.: **African Philosophy.** Myth and Reality, London: Hutchinson, 1983 ([1]1976)

Hughes, John A: **The Philosophy of Social Research**, London: Longman, [2]1990 ([1]1980)

Husen, Torsten/ Postlethwaite, T.Neville (eds.): **The International Encyclopedia of Education.** Research and Studies, 10 vols. Oxford: Pergamon 1985

Husain, S. Abid: **The way of Gandhi and Nehru**, Bombay: Asia, [2]1961 ([1]1959)

Hussain, Zakir: **Education Reconstruction in India.** Sardar Vallabhai Patel Lectures (1958), New Delhi: Government of India, 1959

Illich, Ivan: **Deschooling Society**, New York: Harper & Row, 1971

Illich, Ivan: **Celebration of Awareness.** A Call for Institutional Revolution, Harmondsworth: Penguin, 1978 ([1]1974)

Illich, Ivan: **Toward a History of Need**, New York: Bantam, 1980 ([1]1947)

Iyer, Raghavan: **The Moral and Political Thought of Mahatma Gandhi**, London: Concord Grove Press, [2]1983 ([1]1973)

Jha, Akhileshwar: **The Imprisoned Mind.** Guru-Shishya Tradition in Indian Culture, Delhi: Chanakya, [2]1989 ([1]1980)

Joshi, Shashi: Religion and Marxism. Some Theoretical Problems, **Economic and Political Weekly**, November 9, 1991, pp. 2563-2568

Kalansuriya, A.D.P.: The Buddha and Wittgenstein : A Brief Philosophical Exegesis. **Asian Philosophy**, 3 (1993) 2, pp. 103-111

Kamat, A.R. : **Education and Social Change in India**, Bombay: Somaiya Publications, 1985

(Kant, Immanuel): **The Philosophy of Kant.** Immanuel Kant's Moral and Political Writings, ed. by C.J. Friedrich, New York: Random House, 1977 ([1]1949)

Kant, Immanuel: **Fundamental Principles of the Metaphysics of Morals,** in: Great Books of the Western World, Vol 42: **Kant,** Chicago: Encyclopaedia Britannica, 1982 ([1]1952), pp. 251-287

Kennick, W.E.: Philosophy as Grammar and the Reality of Universals, in: Alice Ambrose/Morris Lazerowitz (eds.): **Ludwig Wittgenstein.** Philosophy and Language, London: Allen & Unwin, 1972, pp. 140-185

Khanna, Suman: **Gandhi and the Good Life,** New Delhi: Gandhi Peace Foundation, 1985

Kripalani, J.B.: **Gandhi**, His Life and Thought, New Delhi; Ministry of Information and Broadcasting, Government of India, 1991 ([1]1970)

Krishna, Daya: **Social Philosophy.** Past and Future, Simla: Indian Institute of Advanced Study, 1969

Krishna, Daya: **The Art of the Conceptual.** Explorations in a Conceptual Maze Over Three Decades, New Delhi: Indian Council of Philosophical Research, 1989

Kumar, Krishna: Profiles of Educators - Mohandas Karamchand Gandhi (1869-1948). **Prospects**, 19 (1989) 4, pp. 591-596

Kumar, Krishna: **Political Agenda of Education.** A Study of Colonialist and Nationalist Ideas, New Delhi: Sage, 1991

Lai, Whalen: The Public Good that does the Public Good: A New Reading of Mohism. **Asian Philosophy**, 3 (1993) 2, pp. 125-141

Lacey. A.R.: **A Dictionary of Philosophy**, London: Routledge & Kegan Paul, [2]1986 ([1]1976)

Larrain, Jorge: **The Concept of Ideology**, New Delhi: B.I. Publications, 1981 ([1]1979)

Lee, Gordon C.: **Education and Democratic Ideals.** Philosophical Backgrounds of Modern Educational Thought, New York: Harcourt, Brace & World, 1965

Lee, Jee-Hun/Wringe, Colin: Rational Autonomy, Morality and Education. **Journal of Philosophy of Education**, 27 (1993) 1, pp. 69-78

Leibowitz, Jeshajahu: **Gespräche über Gott and die Welt** (Talks about God and the World), Frankfurt: Dvorah 1990 ([1]1987)

Leirman, Walter: Adult Education: Movement and Discipline between the Golden Sixties and the Iron Eighties, in: Walter Leirman/Jindra Kulich (eds.): **Adult Education and the Challenges of the 1990s**, London: Croom Helm, 1987, pp. 1-28

Livingstone, David et al: **Critical Pedagogy and Cultural Power**, London: Macmillan, 1987

Macdonell, Diane: **Theories of Discourse.** An Introduction, Oxford: Basil Blackwell, 1989 ([1]1986)

MacIntyre, Alasdair: **After Virtue.** A Study in Moral Theory, London: Gerald Duckworth, 1981

Mackie, Fiona: **The status of everyday life.** A sociological excavation of the prevailing framework of perception, London: Routledge & Kegan Paul, 1985

Mahadevan, T.K.: An Approach to the Study of Gandhi, in : S.C. Biswas (ed.): **Gandhi. Theory and Practice.** Social Impact and Contemporary Relevance. Proceedings of a Seminar, Simla: Indian Institute of Advanced Study, 1969, pp. 45-61

Mahadevan, T.K.: **Gandhi My Refrain.** Controversial Essays: 1950-1972, Bombay: Popular Prakashan, 1973

Mahadevan, T.K.: Gandhi - A Modernist Heresy, in; Donald H. Bishop (ed.): **Indian Thought.** An Introduction, New Delhi: Wiley Eastern, 1975, pp. 357-363

Malhotra, S.L. : A Study of Gandhi's Autobiography, in V.T. Patil (ed.): **New Dimensions and Perspectives in Gandhism**, New Delhi: Inter-India Publcations, 1989, pp. 495-511

Malkani. G.R.: Freedom through Knowledge, in: S. Radhakrishnan/ J.H. Muirhead (eds.): **Contemporary Indian Philosophy,** London: Allen & Unwin, 1982 ([1]1936), pp. 409-428

Marcel, Anthony, J. : Phenomenal experience and functionalism, in: A.J. Marcel/ E. Bisiach (eds.): **Consciousness in Contemporary Science,** Oxford: Clarendon, 1992 ([1]1988)

Maritian, Jacques: **True Humanism,** New York: Scribner's, 1938

Marsella, Anthony J.: Devos, George/Hsu, Francis, L.K. (eds.): **Culture and Self.** Asian and

Western Perspectives, New York: Tavistock, 1985, pp. 185-230

Martirani, Giuliana: Collective Self-Education for Peace. **Gandhi Marg**, 6 (1984) 4 & 5, pp. 385-403

Mathur, D.B.: **Gandhi and the Liberal Bequest**, Jaipur: Aalekh, 1988

Mathur, D.C.: Ends and Means: The Theoretic Foundations of Gandhiji's Ethical Philosophy, in: Kewal Krishan Mittal (ed.): **Ethical Ideas of Mahatma Gandhi** (Seminar Papers and Discussion): Delhi: Gandhi Bhavan, University of Delhi, 1981, pp. 17-25. 25-28

Mathur, S.S.: Researches in Philosophies of Education, in: Y.P. Aggarwal (ed.): **Research in Emerging Fields of Education.** Concepts, Trends and Prospects, New Delhi: Sterling, 1988

Mayo, Bernard: **The Philosophy of Right and Wrong.** An Introduction to Ethical Theory; London: Routledge & Kegan Paul, 1986

Mazumdar, Amiya Kumar: N. V. Banerjee Looks at Education, in: Margaret Chatterjee (ed.): **The Philosophy of Nikunja Vihari Banerjee**, New Delhi: Indian Council of Philosophical Research, 1990

Mehta, J.K.: **Gandhian Thought.** An Analytical Study, New Delhi: Ashish, 1985

Mehta, Rohit: **J.Krishnamurti and the Nameless Experience.** A Comprehensive Discussion of J. Krishnamurti's Approach to Life, Delhi: Motilal Banarsidass, [3]1991 ([1]1979)

Menze. Clemens: Educational Humanism in the Current Discussion. **Education** (A Biannual Collection of Recent German Contributions to the

Field of Educational Research), vol. 44, 1991, pp. 75-87

Miller, Donald F.: **The Reason of Metaphor.** A Study in Politics, New Delhi: Sage, 1992

Mittal, Kewal Krishan (ed.): **Ethical Ideas of Mahatma Gandhi** (Seminar Papers and Discussion), Delhi: Gandhi Bhavan, University of Delhi, 1981

Mohanty, Malaya Kumar: Naturalistic Trends in Gandhian Education. **Gandhi Marg,** 10 (1988) 3, pp. 149-155

Monk, Ray: **Ludwig Wittgenstein.** The Duty of Genius, London: Vintage 1991

Moder, Paul K./ vander Nat, A. (eds.): **Human Knowledge.** Classical and Contemporary Approaches, New York: O.U.P., 1987

Nanda, B.R.: **Mahatma Gandhi.** A Biography, Delhi: O.U.P., 1982 ([1]1958)

Nanda, B.R.: **Gandhi and his Critics,** Delhi: O.U.P., 1985

Navaratnam, Ratna: **New Frontiers in East-West Philosophies of Education,** Bombay: Orient Longmans, 1958

Needleman, Jacob: **The Heart of Philosophy,** London: Routledge & Kegan Paul, 1983

Newell, R.W.: **Objectivity, Empiricism and Truth,** London: Routledge & Kegan Paul, 1986

Niebuhr, Reinhold: **Moral Man and Immoral Society.** A Study in Ethics and Politics, New York, Scribner's, 1960 ([1]1932)

Nitin, M.B.: The Concept of Man in Marxist Thought, in: S. Radhakrishnan/ P.T. Raju (eds.):

The Concept of Man. A Study in Comparative Philosophy, Delhi: Motilal Banarsidass, 1992 ([1]1966)

Oxford English Dictionary, The, Oxford: Clarendon Press, 1989

Pani, Ragunath: **Integral Education: Thought and Practice**, New Delhi: Ashish 1987

Panikkar, Raimundo: **The Unknown Christ in Hinduism.** Towards an Ecumenical Christophany, London: Darton, Longman & Todd, [2]1981 ([1]1964)

Pantham, Thomas: Some Dimensions of the Universality of Philosophical Hermeneutics: A Conversation with Hans Georg Gadamer. **Journal of Indian Council of Philosophical Research**, 9 (1992) 3, pp. 132-135

Papineau, David: **For Science in the Social Sciences,** London: Macmillan, 1978

Parekh, Bhikhu: Some Puzzles about Gandhi's Autobiography, in: Ramashray Roy (eds.): **Contemporary Crisis and Gandhi,** New Delhi: Discovery, 1986, pp. 14-30

Parekh, Bhikhu/Pantham, Thomas (ed.): **Political Discourse**. Explorations in Indian and Western Political Thought, New Delhi: Sage, 1987

Parekh, Bhikhu: **Gandhi's Political Philosophy**. A Critical Examination. London: Macmillan, 1989 (a)

Parekh, Bhikhu: **Colonialism, Tradition and Reform.** An Analysis of Gandhi's Political Discourse, New Delhi Sage, 1989 (b)

Parel, Anthony J.: Keith, Ronald C. (eds.): **Comparative Political Philosophy.** Studies under the Upas Tree, New Delhi Sage, 1992

Patel, C.N.: **Mahatma Gandhi in his Gujarati Writings**, New Delhi: Sahitya Akademi, 1981

Patel, M.S.: **The Educational Philosophy of Mahatma Gandhi**, Ahmedabad: Navajivan, 1959 ([1]1953)

Pears, David: Predicting and Deciding, in: P.F. Strawson (ed.): **Studies in the Philosophy of Thought and Action**, London: O.U.P., 1968

Pflug, Bernd: **Education in Ayurveda.** A Re-constructional Analysis, New Delhi: Gyan, 1992

Pflug, Bernd: Who is Afraid of the Unknown? **Radical Humanist**, 57 (1993) 3, pp. 6-7

Pillai, N.P. : **The Educational Aims of Mahatma Gandhi**, Trivandrum: Kalyanmandir Publications, 1959

Place, U.T: On the social relativity of truth and the analytic/synthetic distinction. **Human Studies**, 14 (1991) 4, pp. 265-285

Popper, Karl R.: **Conjectures And Refutations.** The Growth of Scientific Knowledge, London: Routledge & Kegan Paul, 1985 ([1]1963)

Prasad, Rajendra: **Karma, Causation and Retributive Morality**, Conceptual Essays in Ethics and Metaethics, New Delhi: Indian Council of Philosophical Research, 1989 (a)

Prasad, Rajendra (ed.): **Ends and Means in Private and Public Life**, Shimla: Indian Institute of Advanced Study, 1989 (b)

Radhakrishnan, N. (ed.): **Gandhian Perspective of Nation Building for World Peace**, New Delhi: Konark, 1992

Ramachandra, G.P.: **Re-Experiencing Past Thoughts.** Paper presented to the workshop on New

Trends in Historical Methodology, Mahatma Gandhi University, Kottayam, Kerala, 18-29 January 1994 (mimeographed)

Rassekh, S./ Vaideanu, G.: **The contents of education.** A worldwide view of their development from the present to the year 2000, New Delhi: Sterling, 1989 ([1]1987)

Rattan, Ram: **Gandhi's Thought & Action,** Delhi: Kalinga, 1991

Ray, B.G.: Humanism and Nationalism, in: K.K. Mittal (ed.): **Nationalism and Humanism** (Seminar Papers and Discussion), Delhi: Gandhi Bhavan, University of Delhi, 1981, pp. 6-11

Richards, Glyn: **The Philosophy of Gandhi.** A study of his basic ideas, Calcutta: Rupa, 1991

Rippa, S. Alexander: **Education in a free Society.** An American History, New York: Longman, [6]1988 ([1]1967)

Rorty, Richard: Contingency, irony, and solidarity, Cambridge: O.U.P., 1989

Rorty, Richard: A Pragmatist View of Rationality and Cultural Difference. **Philosophy East & West,** 42 (1992) 4, pp. 581-596

Roy, Krishna/Gupta, Chhanda (eds.): **Essays in Social and Political Philosophy,** New Delhi: Indian Council of Philosophical Research, 1989

Roy, M.N.: **Scientific Politics,** Calcutta: Renaissance, [2]1947 ([1]1942)

Roy, M.N.: **Politics, Power and Parties,** Delhi: Ajanta, 1981 ([1]1960) (a)

Roy, M.N.: **New Humanism.** A Manifesto. Delhi: Ajanta, 1981 ([1] 1939) (b)

Roy, M.N. **Men I met,** Delhi: Ajanta, 1981 ([1]1968) (c)

Roy M.N.: **Science and Philosophy,** Delhi: Ajanta, 1984 ([1]1947)

Roy, M.N.: **Reason, Romanticism and Revolution,** Delhi: Ajanta, 1989 ([1]1952 - vol. 1, 1955 -vol. 2)

Roy, Ramashray: **Self and Society.** A Study in Gandhian Thought, New Delhi: Sage, 1984

Russell, Bertrand: **Mysticism and Logic,** London: Unwin, 1989 ([1]1917)

Ryle, Gilbert: "If," "So," and "Because", in: Max Black (ed.): **Philosophical Analysis.** A Collection of Essays, Englewod Cliffs: Prentice-Hall, 1963, pp. 302-318

Saiyidain, K.G.: **Education, Culture and the Social Order,** Bombay: Asia, [2]1963 ([1]1952)

Saiyidain, K.G.: Universities and the Life of the Mind, Bombay: Asia, 1965 (a)

Saiyidain, K.G.: **The Faith of an Educationist,** A Plea for Humane Values, Bombay: Asia, 1965 (b)

Saiyidain, K.G.: The Educationist, in: B.K. Ahluwalia/ Shashi Ahluwalia (eds.): **Facets of Gandhi,** New Delhi: Indian Academic Publishers, n.d. (c. 1981)

Salamatullah: Basic Education: A Case Study, in: P.R. Panchamukhi (ed.): **Studies in Educational Reform in India** (5 vols.), vol. 2: Educational Reforms at Different Levels, Bombay: Himalaya, 1989, pp. 3-53

Sarin, Indu/Goel, D.: Value Intention and Action, in: S.R. Bhatt (ed.): **Reality, Knowledge and**

Value, Delhi: Bharatiya Vidya Prakashan, 1985, pp. 53-58

Sartre, Jean-Paul: **Existentialism and Humanism**, London: Methuen, 1949 ([1]1946)

Saxena, S.K.: The Fabric of Self-Suffering: A Study in Gandhi, in: Kapil N. Tiwari (ed.): **Suffering: Indian Perspectives,** Delhi: Motilal Banarsidass, 1986, pp. 226-236

Saxena, Sushil Kumar: **Ever Unto God.** Essays on Gandhi and Religion, New Delhi: Indian Council of Philosophical Research, 1988

Schafritz, Jay M./Koeppe, Richard P./Sopher, Elizabeth W.: **The Fact of File Dictionary of Education**, New York: Facts on File, 1988

Schmidtz, David: **Choosing Ends. Ethics**, 104 (1994) 2, pp. 226-251

Schoeck, Helmut/Wiggings, James W. (eds.): **Relativism and the Study of Man,** Prinception: D. Van Nostrand, 1961

Seetharamu, A. S.: **Philosophies of Education**, New Delhi: Ashish, 1989

Sengupta, Pradip Kumar (ed.): **Freedom, Transcendence and Identity**, New Delhi: Indian Council of Philosophical Research, 1988

Sethi, J.D.: Gandhian Values and the 20th Century Challenges. Patel Memorial Lectures - 1979, in: Government of India (ed.): **Patel Memorial Lectures (1955-1985),** New Delhi: Ministry of Information and Broadcasting, 1990, pp. 1141-1186

Sharma, Rameshwar: Continuing Education of the Medical Profession in India, in: A. Bordia/ J.R.Kidd/J.A. Draper (eds.): **Adult Education in**

India. A Book of Readings, Bombay: Nachiketa, 1973, pp. 357-361

Sharma, Shiv: **The System of Ayurveda**,Delhi: Neeraj, 1983 ([1]1929)

Shivarudrappa, G.: **Philosophical Approach to Education,** Bombay: Himalaya, 1985

Silver, Harold: **Education and the Social Condition,** London: Methuen, 1980

Sinari: Ramakant A.: **The Structure of Indian Thought,** Delhi: O.U.P. 1984 ([1]1970)

Sinari, Ramakant (ed.): **Concept of Man in Philosophy**, Shimla: Indian Institute of Advanced Study, 1991

Singh, Ramjee: **Gandhi and the Modern World,** New Delhi: Classical Publishing Company, 1988

Singh, Ramjee: **Gandhi and the Twenty-First Century,** New Delhi: Peace Publishers, 1993

Singh, Randhir: **Reason, Revolution and Political Theory.** Notes on Michael Oakeshott's "Rationalism in Politics", Delhi: Ajanta, [3]1988 ([1]1967)

Singh, Samporan: **The Holistic Education,** New Delhi: Siddarth, 1987

Solomon, Robert C.: Existentialism, Emotions, and the Cultural Limits of Rationality. **Philosophy East & West,** 42 (1992) 4, pp. 597-621

Spratt, P.: Gandhi and the Communists, in Sibnarayan Ray (ed.): **Gandhi, India and the World.** An International Symposium, Bombay: Nachiketa, 1970 pp. 197-209

Srinivasan, G.: Levels of Self-Knowledge and Self-Indentity, **Indian Philosophical Annual**, vol. 20 1987-88. pp. 29-37

Standish, Paul: Educational Discourse: meaning and mythology. **Journal of Philosophy of Education**, 25 (1991) 2, pp.171-182

Tarkunde, V.M.: **Radical Humanism.** The Philosophy of Freedom and Democracy, Delhi: Ajanta, 1983

Tattvartha Sutra. That Which Is. Umasvati/ Umasvami with the combined Commentaries of Umasvati/ Umasvami, Pajyapada and Siddhasenagani. Translated with an introduction by Nathmal Tatia. New York: Harper Collins, 1994

Tendulkar, D.G.: **Mahatma.** Life of Mohandas Karamchand Gandhi (8 vols), vol.4: 1934-1938, Delhi: Ministry of Information & Broadcasting, 1961 ([1]1952)

Terchek, Ronald J.: Gandhi and Democratic Theory, in: Thomas Pantham/Kenneth L. Deutsch (eds.): **Political Thought in Modern India**, New Delhi: Sage, 1986, pp. 307-324

Titmus, Colin: Comparative Approach to Adult Education. **International Journal of University Adult Education**, 28 (1989) 3, p. 1-12

Thomson, Mark : **Gandhi and his Ashrams**, Bombay: Popular Prakashan, 1993

Usher, Robin: Experience in Adult Education: a post-modern critique. **Journal of Philosophy of Education**, 26 (1992) 2, pp. 201-214

Visvanathan, Shiv: Autobiography as experiment. **Seminar**, No.409, September 1993, pp.12-15

Vinoba: **Thoughts on Education**, Varanasi: Sarva Seva Sangh Prakashan, [3]1985

Wain, Kenneth: Lifelong Education: a duty to oneself? **Journal of Philosophy of Education**, 25 (1991) 2, pp. 273-278

Wenham, Martin: Education as Interaction. **Journal of Philosophy of Education,** 25 (1991) 2, 235-245

White, Patricia: **Beyond Domination.** An Essay in the Political Philosophy of Education, London: Routledge & Kegan Paul, 1983

Whitehead, Alfred North: **The Aims of Education** and Other Essays, New York: The Free Press, 1967 ([1]1929)

Williams, Bernard: The need to be sceptical, in: **Times Literary Supplement**, February 16-22, 1990, pp. 163-164

Wilson, Edgar: **The Mental as Physical,** London: Routledge & Kegan Paul, 1979

Wingo, G. Max: **Philosophies of Education:** An Introduction, New Delhi: Sterling, 1975

Wlodkowski, Raymond J.: Instructional Design and Learner Motivation, in: Kerry A. Johnson/Lin J.Foa (eds.): **Instructional Design.** New Alternatives for Effective Education and Training, New York: Macmillan, 1989

Wulf, Christoph: Self-Education: An Essential Element of Education. **Education,** Vol. 26 1982, pp. 13-19

Wynne, John P.: **Theories of Education.** An Introduction to the Foundations of Education, New York: Harper & Row, 1963

Yadav, Yogendra: Four Questions for Gandhians. Review Essay. **Lokayan Bulletin,** 10:2, 1993, pp. 37-42

Zaidi, Sabira K.: **Education and Humanism.** A Collection of Essays, Simla: Indian Institute of Advanced Study, 1971

Index